HOW TO WRITE A NOVEL
A PRACTICAL GUIDE TO THE ART OF FICTION

MJP
PUBLISHERS

HOW TO WRITE A NOVEL
A PRACTICAL GUIDE TO THE ART OF FICTION

G. Richards

MJP
PUBLISHERS

Chennai　　　Trichy　　　Tirunelveli　　　New Delhi

MJP PUBLISHERS

ISBN 978-81-8094-328-7   **MJP Publishers**

All rights reserved   No. 44, Nallathambi Street,

Printed and bound in India   Triplicane, Chennai 600 005

MJP   299   © Publishers, 2019

Publisher :   **C. Janarthanan**

Project Editor :   **C. Ambica**

Publisher's Note

The legacy of a country is in its varied cultural heritage, historical literature, developments in the field of economy and science. The top nations in the world are competing in the field of science, economy and literature. This vast legacy has to be conserved and documented so that it can be bestowed to the future generation. The knowledge of this legacy is slowly getting perished in the present generation due to lack of documentation.

Keeping this in mind, the concern with retrospective acquiring of rare books has been accented recently by the burgeoning reprint industry. MJP Publishers is gratified to retrieve the rare collections with a view to bring back those books that were landmarks in their time.

In this effort, a series of rare books would be republished under the banner, "MJP Publishers". The books in the reprint series have been carefully selected for their contemporary usefulness as well as their historical importance within the intellectual. We reconstruct the book with slight enhancements made for better presentation, without affecting the contents of the original edition.

Most of the works selected for republishing covers a huge range of subjects, from history to anthropology. We believe this reprint edition will be a service to the numerous researchers and practitioners active in this fascinating field. We allow readers to experience the wonder of peering into a scholarly work of the highest order and seminal significance.

MJP Publishers

Preface

This little book is one which so well explains itself th
no introductory word is needed; and I only venture
intrude a sentence or two here with a view to explain th
style in which I have conveyed my ideas. I desired to b
plain and practical, and therefore chose the direct an
epistolary form as being most suitable for the purpose i
hand.

Contents

Chapter I

The Object in View

I am setting myself a task which some people would call very ambitious; others would call it by a name not quite so polite; and a considerable number would say it was positively absurd, accompanying their criticism with derisive laughter. Having discussed the possibility of teaching the art of writing fiction with a good many different kinds of people, I know quite intimately the opinions which are likely to be expressed about this little book; and although I do not intend to burden the reader with an account of their respective merits, I do intend to make my own position as clear as possible. First of all, I will examine the results of a recent symposium on the general question.[1] When asked as to the practicability of a School of Fiction, Messrs Robert Barr, G. Manville Fenn, M. Betham Edwards, Arthur Morrison, G. B. Burgin, C. J. C. Hyne, and "Mr" John Oliver Hobbes declared against it; Miss Mary L. Pendered and Miss Clementina Black—with certain reservations—spoke in favour of such an institution. True, these names do not include all representatives of the high places in Fiction, but they are quite respectable enough for my purpose. It will be seen that the vote is adverse to the object I have in view. Why?

1. *The New Century Review*, **vol. i.**

Well, here are a few reasons. Mr Morrison affirms that writing as a trade is far too pleasant an idea; John Oliver Hobbes is of opinion that it is impossible to teach anyone how to produce a work of imagination; and Mr G. B. Burgin asserts that genius is its own teacher—a remark characterised by unwitting modesty. Now, with the spirit of these convictions I am not disposed to quarrel. This is an age which imagines that everything can be crammed into the limits of an academical curriculum; and there are actually some people who would not hesitate to endow a chair of "Ideas and Imagination." We need to be reminded occasionally that there are incommunicable elements in all art.

AN INEVITABLE COMPARISON

But the question arises: If there be an art of literature, why cannot its principles be taught and practised as well as those of any other art? We have schools of Painting, Sculpture, and Music—why not a school of Fiction? Let it be supposed that a would-be artist has conceived a brilliant idea which he is anxious to embody in literature or put on a canvas. In order to do so, he must observe certain well-established rules which we may call the grammar of art: for just as in literature a man may express beautiful ideas in ungrammatical language, and without any sense of relationship or development, so may the same ideas be put in a picture, and yet the art be of the crudest. Now, in what way will our would-be artist become acquainted with those rules? The answer is simple. If his genius had

been of the first order he would have known them intuitively: the society of men and women, of great books
and fine pictures, would have provided sufficient stimuli
to bring forth the best productions of his mind. Thus
Shakespeare was never taught the principles of dramatic
art; Bach had an instinctive appreciation of the laws of
harmony; and Turner had the same insight into laws of
painting. These were artists of the front rank: they simply
looked—and understood.

But if his powers belonged to the order which is
called *talent*, he would have to do one of two things: either stumble upon these rules one by one and learn them
by experience—or be taught them in their true order by
others, in which case an Institute of Literary Art would
already exist in an embryonic stage. Why should it not
be developed into a matured school? Is it that the dignity
of genius forbids it, or that pupilage is half a disgrace?
True genius never shuns the marks of the learner. Even
Shakespeare grew in the understanding of art and in his
power of handling its elements. Professor Dowden says:
"In the 'Two Gentlemen of Verona,' Porteus, the fickle, is
set over against Valentine the faithful; Sylvia, the bright
and intellectual, is set over against Julia, the ardent and
tender; Launce, the humorist, is set over against Speed,
the wit. This indicates a certain want of confidence on the
part of the poet; he fears the weight of too much liberty.
He cannot yet feel that his structure is secure without a
mechanism to support the structure. He endeavours to
attain unity of effect less by the inspiration of a common

life than by the disposition of parts. In the early plays structure determines function; in the later plays organisation is preceded by life."[2]

A MODEL LESSON IN NOVEL-WRITING

When certain grumpy folk ask: "How do you propose to draw up your lessons on 'The way to find Local Colour'; 'Plotting'; 'How to manage a Love-Scene,' and so forth?" it is expected that a writer like myself will be greatly disconcerted. Not at all. It so happens that a distinguished critic, now deceased, once delivered himself on the possibility of teaching literary art, and I propose to quote a paragraph or two from his article. "The morning finds the master in his working arm-chair; and seated about the room which is generally the study, but is now the studio, are some half-dozen pupils. The subject for the hour is narrative-construction, and the master holds in his hand a small MS. which, as he slowly reads it aloud, proves to be a somewhat elaborate synopsis of the story of one of his own published or projected novels. The reading over, students are free to state objections, or to ask questions. One remarks that the *dénouement* is brought about by a mere accident, and therefore seems to lack the inevitableness which, the master has always taught, is essential to organic unity. The criticism is recognised as intelligent, but the master shows that the accident has not the purely fortuitous character which renders it obnoxious to the general objection. While it is technically an accident, it is in reality hardly accidental, but an oc-

---

2.   "Shakespeare: His Mind and Art," p. 61.

currence which fits naturally into an opening provided by a given set of circumstances, the circumstances having been brought about by a course of action which is vitally characteristic of the person whose fate is involved. Then the master himself will ask a question. 'The students,' he says, 'will have noticed that a character who takes no important part in the action until the story is more than half told, makes an insignificant and unnoticeable appearance in a very early chapter, where he seems a purposeless and irrelevant intrusion.' They have paper before them, and he gives them twenty minutes in which to state their opinion as to whether this premature appearance is, or is not, justified by the canons of narrative art, giving, of course, the reasons upon which that opinion has been formed. The papers are handed in to be reported upon next morning, and the lesson is at an end."[3]

This is James Ashcroft Noble's idea of handling a theme in fiction; one of a large and varied number. To me it is a feasible plan emanating from a man who was the sanest of literary advisers. If it be objected that Mr Noble was only a critic and not a novelist, perhaps a word from Sir Walter Besant may add the needful element of authority. "I can conceive of a lecturer dissecting a work, or a series of works, showing how the thing sprang first from a central figure in a central group; how there arose about this group, scenery, the setting of the fable; how the atmosphere became presently charged with the presence of mankind, other characters attaching themselves to the group; how situations, scenes, conversations, led up

3. Article in *The New Age.*

little by little to the full development of this central idea. I can also conceive of a School of Fiction in which the students should be made to practise observation, description, dialogue, and dramatic effects. The student, in fact, would be taught how to use his tools." A reading-class for the artistic study of great writers could not be other than helpful. One lesson might be devoted to the way in which the best authors foreshadowed crises and important turns in events. An example may be found in "Julius Cæsar," where, in the second scene, the soothsayer says:

"Beware the Ides of March!"

—a solitary voice in strange contrast with those by whom he is surrounded, and preparing us for the dark deed upon which the play is based. Or the text-book might be a modern novel—Hardy's "Well-Beloved" for instance—a work full of delicate literary craftsmanship. The storm which overtook Pierston and Miss Bencomb is prepared for—first by the conversation of two men who pass them on the road, and one of whom casually remarks that the weather seems likely to change; then Pierston himself observes "the evening—louring"; finally, and most suddenly, the rain descends in perfect fury.

THE TEACHABLE AND THE UNTEACHABLE

I hope my position is now beginning to be tolerably clear to the reader. I address myself to the man or woman of talent—those people who have writing ability, but who need instruction in the manipulation of characters, the formation of plots, and a host of other points with which

I shall deal hereafter. As to what is teachable, and not teachable, in writing novels, perhaps I may be permitted to use a close analogy. Style, *per se*, is absolutely unteachable simply because it is the man himself; you cannot teach *personality*. Can Dickens, Thackeray, and George Meredith be reduced to an academic schedule? Never. Every soul of man is an individual entity and cannot be reproduced. But although style is incommunicable, the writing of easy, graceful English can be taught in any class-room—that is to say, the structure of sentences and paragraphs, the logical sequence of thought, and the secret of forceful expression are capable of exact scientific treatment.

In like manner, although no school could turn out novelists to order—a supply of Stevensons annually, and a brace of Hardys every two years—there is yet enough common material in all art-work to be mapped out in a course of lessons. I shall show that the two great requisites of novel-writing are (1) a good story to tell, and (2) ability to tell it effectively. Briefly stated, my position is this: no teaching can produce "good stories to tell," but it can increase the power of "the telling," and change it from crude and ineffective methods to those which reach the apex of developed art. Of course there are dangers to be avoided, and the chief of them is that mechanical correctness, "so praiseworthy and so intolerable," as Lowell says in his essay on Lessing. But this need not be an insurmountable difficulty. A truly educated man never labours to speak correctly; being educated, grammatical language follows as a necessary consequence. The same is true of the artist: when he has learned the secrets of literature, he puts away all thoughts of rule and law—nay, in time, his very ideas assume artistic form.

Chapter II

A Good Story to Tell

WHERE DO NOVELISTS GET THEIR STORIES FROM?

I said a moment ago that no teaching could impart a story. If you cannot invent one for yourself, by observation of life and sympathetic insight into human nature, you may depend upon it that you are not called to be a writer of novels. Then where, it may be asked, do novelists get their stories? Well, they hardly know themselves; they say the ideas "come." For instance, here is the way Mr Baring Gould describes the advent of "Mehalah." "One day in Essex, a friend, a captain in the coastguard, invited me to accompany him on a cruise among the creeks in the estuary of the Maldon river—the Blackwater. I went out, and we spent the day running among mud flats and low holms, covered with coarse grass and wild lavender, and startling wild-fowl. We stopped at a ruined farm built on arches above this marsh to eat some lunch; no glass was in the windows, and the raw wind howled in and swept around us. That night I was laid up with a heavy cold. I tossed in bed and was in the marshes in imagination, listening to the wind and the lap of the tide; and 'Mehalah' naturally rose out of it all, a tragic gloomy tale."[4]

---

4. "The Art of Writing Fiction," p. 43.

Exactly. "Mehalah" *rose*; that is enough! If ideas, plots of stories, and new groupings of character do not "rise" in *your* mind, it is simply because you lack the power to originate them spontaneously. Take the somewhat fabulous story of Newton and the apple. Many a man before Sir Isaac had seen an apple fall, but not one of them used that observation as he did. In the same way there are scores of men who have the same experiences and live the same kind of life, but it occurs to only one among their number to gather up these experiences into an interesting narrative. Why should it "occur" to one and not the others? Because the one has literary gifts and literary impetus, and the others—haven't.

IS THERE A DEEPER QUESTION?

Having dealt with that side of the subject, I should like to say that all novelists have their own methods of obtaining raw material for stories. By raw material I mean those facts of life which give birth to narrative ideas. It is said of Thomas Hardy that he never rides in an omnibus or railway carriage without mentally inventing the history of every traveller. One has to beware of fables in writing of such men, but I have no reason to doubt the statement just made. I do not make it with the intention of advocating anybody to go and do likewise, but as illustrating one way of studying human nature and developing the imaginative faculty.

It will be necessary to speak of *observation* a good many times in the course of these remarks, and one

might as well say what the word really means. Does it
mean "seeing things"? A great deal more than that. It is
very easy to "see things" and yet not observe at all. If you
want ideas for stories, or characters with which to form
a longer narrative, you must not only use your *eyes* but
your *mind*. What is wanted is *observation* with *inference*;
or, to be more correct, with*imagination*. Make sure that
you know the traits of character that are typically human;
those which are the same in a Boer, a Hindu, or a Chi-
naman. It is not difficult to mark the special points of
each of these as distinct from the Englishman; but your
first duty is to know human nature *per se*. How is that
knowledge to be obtained? do you say! Well, begin with
yourself; there is ample scope in that direction. And when
you are tired of looking within—look without. Enter a
tram-car and listen to the people talking. Who talks the
loudest? What kind of woman is it who always gives the
conductor most trouble? The man who sits at the far end
of the car in a shabby coat, and who is regarding his boots
with a fixed, anxious stare—what is he thinking about?
and what is his history? Then a baby begins to yell, and its
mother cannot soothe it. One old man smiles benignly on
the struggling infant, but the old man next to him looks
"daggers." And why?

To see character in action there is no finer van-
tage-point than the top of a London omnibus. Watch the
way in which people walk; notice their forms of salutation
when they meet; and study the expressions on their faces.
Tragedy and comedy are everywhere, and you have not
to go beneath the surface of life in order to find them. It

sounds prosaic enough to speak of studying human nature at a railway station, but such places are brimful of event. I know more than one novelist who has found his "motif" by quietly watching the crowd on a platform from behind a waiting-room window. Wherever humanity congregates there should the student be. Not that he should restrict his observations to men and women in groups or masses—he must cover all the ground by including individuals who are to be specially considered. The logician's terms come in handy at this point: *extensive* and *intensive*—such must be the methods of a beginner's analysis of his fellow-creatures.

WHAT ABOUT THE NEWSPAPERS?

The daily press is the great mirror of human events. When we open the paper at our breakfast table we find a literal record of the previous day's joy and sorrow—marriages and murders, failures and successes, news from afar and news from the next street—they all find a place. The would-be novel writer should be a diligent student of the newspaper. In no other sphere will he discover such a plenitude of raw material. Some of the cases tried at the Courts contain elements of dramatic quality far beyond those he has ever imagined; and here and there may be found in miniature the outlines of a splendid plot. Of course everything depends on the reader's mind. If you cannot read between the lines—that is the end of the matter, and your novel will remain unwritten; but if you can—some day you may expect to succeed.

I once came across a practical illustration of the manner in which a newspaper paragraph was treated imaginatively. The result is rather crude and unfinished, but most likely it was never intended to stand as a finished production, occurring as it does, in an American book on American journalism.[5]

Here is the paragraph:

"John Simpson and Michael Flannagan, two railroad labourers, quarrelled yesterday morning, and Flannagan killed Simpson with a coupling-pin. The murderer is in jail. He says Simpson provoked him and dared him to strike."

Now the question arises: What was the quarrel about? We don't know; so an originating cause must be invented. The inventor whose illustration I am about to give conceived the story thus:

"'Taint none o' yer business how often I go to see the girl."

"Ef Oi ketch yez around my Nora's house agin, Oi'll break a hole in yer shneakin' head, d'ye moind thot!"

"You braggin' Irish coward, you haint got sand enough in you to come down off'n that car and say that to my face."

It was John Simpson, a yard switchman who spoke this taunt to a section hand. A moment more and Mi-

---

5. Shuman, "Steps into Journalism," p. 208.

chael Flannagan stood on the ground beside him. There was a murderous fire in the Irishman's eyes, and in his hand he held a heavy coupling-pin.

"Tut! tut! Mike. Throw away the iron and play fair. You can wallup him!" cried the rest of the gang.

"He's a coward; he dassn't hit me," came the wasp-like taunt of the switchman. "Let him alone, fellers; his girl's give him the shake, and——"

Those were the last words Simpson spoke. The murderous coupling-pin had descended like a scimitar and crushed his skull.

An awed silence fell upon the little group as they raised the fallen man and saw that he was dead.

"Ye'll be hangin' fur this, Mikey, me bye," whispered one of his horrified companions as the police dragged off the unresisting murderer.

"Oi don't care," came the sullen reply, with a dry sob that belied it. Then, with a look of unutterable hatred, and a nod towards the white, upturned face of his enemy, he added under his breath, "He'll niver git her now."

This is enough to give the beginner an idea of the way in which stories and plots sometimes "occur" to writers of fiction. It is, however, only one of a thousand ways, and my advice to the novice is this: Keep your eyes and ears open; observe and inquire, read and reflect; look at life and the things of life from your own point of view;

and just as a financier manipulates events for the sake of money, so ought you to turn all your experiences into the mould of fiction. If, after this, you don't succeed, it is evident you have made a mistake. Be courageous enough to acknowledge the fact, and leave the writing of novels to others.

Chapter III

How to Begin

You have now obtained your story—in its bare outlines, at least. The next question is, How are you to make a start? Well, that is an important question, and it cannot be evaded.

Clarence Rook, in a waggish moment, said two things were necessary in order to write a novel:

(1) *Writing Materials*,

(2) *A Month*;

but he seems to have thought that the month should be a month's imprisonment for attempting such an indiscretion. In these pages, however, we are serious folk, and having thanked Mr Rook for his pleasantry, we return to the point before us.

First of all, What kind of a novel is yours to be? Historical? If so, have you read all the authorities? Do you feel the throb of the life of that period about which you are going to write? Are its chief personages living beings in your imagination? and have you learned all the details respecting customs, manners, language, and dress? If not, you are very far from being ready to make a start, even though the "story" itself is quite clear to you.

Our great historical novelists devour libraries before they sit down to write. One would like to know how many books Dr Conan Doyle digested before he published "The Refugees," and Stanley Weyman before he brought out his "A Gentleman of France." Do not be carried away with the alluring idea that it is easy to take up historical subjects because the characters are there to hand, and the "story" practically "made." Directly you make the attempt, you will find out your mistake. Write about the life you know best—the life of the present day. You will then avoid the necessity of keeping everything in chronological perspective—a necessity which an open-air preacher, whom I heard last week, quite forgot when he said that the sailors shouted down the hatchway to the sleeping Prophet of Nineveh: "Jonah! We're sinking! Come and help us with the pumps!"

No; before you begin, have a clear idea of what you are going to do. The type of your story will in many cases decide the kind of treatment required; but it may be well, nevertheless, to say a few words about the various kinds of novels that are written nowadays, and the differences that separate them one from another.

There is the *Realistic* novel, of which Mr Maugham's "Liza of Lambeth" and Mr Morrison's "A Child of the Jago" may be taken as recent examples. These authors attempt to picture life as it is; they sink their own personalities, and endeavour to write a literal account of the "personalities" of other people. Very often they succeed, but absolute realism is impossible unless a man has no objection to appearing in a Police Court. In this type of fiction, plot, action, and inter-play of characters are not important: the main purpose is a sort of literary biograph; life in action, without comment or underlying philosophy, and minus the pre-eminent factor of art.

Then there is the novel of *Manners*. The customs of life, the social peculiarities of certain groups of men and women, the humours and moral qualities of life—these are the chief features in the novel of manners. As a form of fiction it is earlier than the realistic novel, but both are alike in having little or no concern with plot and character development.

Next comes the novel of *Incident*. Here the stress is placed upon particular events—what led up to them and the consequences that followed—hence the structure of the narrative, and the powers of movement and suspense are important factors in achieving success.

A *Romance* is in a very important sense a novel of incident, but the "incident" is specialised in character, and usually deals with the passionate and fundamental powers of man—hate, jealousy, revenge, and scenes of violence. Or it may be "incident" which has to do with life in other worlds as imagined by the writer, and occasionally takes on the style of the supernatural.

Lastly, there is the *Dramatic* novel, where the chief feature is the influence of event on character, and of characters on each other.

Now, to which class is your projected novel to belong? In fiction you must walk by sight and not by faith. Never sit down to write believing that although you can't see the finish of your story, it will come out all right "in the end." It won't. You should know at the outset to which type of fiction you are to devote your energies; how, otherwise, can you observe the laws of art which govern its ideal being?

FORMATION OF THE PLOT

In one sense your plot is formed already—that is to say, the very idea of your story involves a plot more or less distinct. As yet, however, you do not see clearly how things are going to work out, and it is now your business to settle the matter so far as it lies in your power to do so. Now, a plot is not *made*; it is *a structural growth*. Suppose you wish to present a domestic scene in which the folly of high temper is to be proved. Is not the plot concealed in the idea? Certainly. Hence you perhaps place a man and his wife at breakfast. They begin to talk amiably, then become quarrelsome, and finally fall into loving agreement. Or you light upon a more original plan of bringing out your point; but in any case, the plot evolves itself step by step. Wilkie Collins has left some interesting gossip behind him with reference to "The Woman in White": "My first proceeding is to get my central idea—the pivot on which the story turns. The central idea in 'The Woman in White' is the idea of a conspiracy in private life, in which circumstances are so handled as to rob a woman of her identity, by confounding her with another woman sufficiently like her in personal appearance to answer the wicked purpose. The destruction of her identity represents a first division of her story; the recovery of her identity marks a second division. My central idea next suggests some of my chief characters.

"A clever devil must conduct the conspiracy. Male devil or female devil? The sort of wickedness wanted seems to be a man's wickedness. Perhaps a foreign man. Count Fosco faintly shows himself to me before I know his name. I let him wait, and begin to think about the two women. They must be both innocent, and both interesting. Lady Glyde dawns on me as one of the innocent victims. I try to discover the other—and fail. I try what a walk will do for me—and fail. I devote the evening to a new effort—and fail. Experience tells me to take no more trouble about it, and leave that other woman to come of her own accord. The next morning before I have been awake in my bed for more than ten minutes, my perverse brains set to work without consulting me. Poor Anne Catherick comes into the room, and says 'Try me.'

"I have now got an idea, and three of my characters. What is there to do now? My next proceeding is to begin building up the story. Here my favourite three efforts must be encountered. First effort: To begin at the beginning. Second effort: To keep the story always advancing, without paying the smallest attention to the serial division in parts, or to the book publications in volumes. Third effort: To decide on the end. All this is done as my father used to paint his skies in his famous sea-pictures—

at one heat. As yet I do not enter into details; I merely set up my landmarks. In doing this, the main situations of the story present themselves in all sorts of new aspects. These discoveries lead me nearer and nearer to finding the right end. The end being decided on, I go back again to the beginning, and look at it with a new eye, and fail to be satisfied with it."

THE AGONIES AND JOYS OF "PLOT-CONSTRUCTION"

"I have yielded to the worst temptation that besets a novelist—the temptation to begin with a striking incident without counting the cost in the shape of explanations that must and will follow. These pests of fiction, to reader and writer alike, can only be eradicated in one way. I have already mentioned the way—to begin at the beginning. In the case of 'The Woman in White,' I get back, as I vainly believe, to the true starting-point of the story. I am now at liberty to set the new novel going, having, let me repeat, no more than an outline of story and characters before me, and leaving the details in each case to the spur of the moment. For a week, as well as I can remember, I work for the best part of every day, but not as happily as usual. An unpleasant sense of something wrong worries me. At the beginning of the second week a disheartening discovery reveals itself. I have not found the right beginning of 'The Woman in White' yet. The scene of my opening chapters is in Cumberland. Miss Fairlie (afterwards Lady Glyde); Mr Fairlie, with his irritable nerves and his art treasures; Miss Halcombe (discovered suddenly, like Anne Catherick), are all waiting the arrival of the young drawing-master, Walter Hartwright. No; this won't do. The person to be first introduced is Anne Catherick. She must already be a familiar figure to the reader when the reader accompanies me to Cumberland. This is what must be done, but I don't see how to do it; no new idea comes to me; I and my MS. have quarrelled, and don't speak to each other. One evening I happen to read of a lunatic who has escaped from an asylum—a paragraph of a few lines only in a newspaper. Instantly the idea comes to me of Walter Hartwright's midnight meeting with Anne Catherick escaped from the asylum. 'The Woman in White' begins again, and nobody will ever be half as much interested in it now as I am. From that moment I have done with my miseries. For the next six months the pen goes on. It is work, hard work; but the harder the better, for this excellent reason: the work is its own exceeding great reward. As an example of the gradual manner in which I reached the development of character, I may return for a moment to Fosco. The making him fat was an afterthought; his canaries and his white mice were found next; and, the most valuable discovery of all, his admiration of Miss Halcombe, took its rise in a conviction that he would not be true to nature unless there was some weak point somewhere in his character."

CARE IN THE USE OF ACTUAL EVENTS

I do not apologise for the lengthiness of this quotation— it is so much to the point, and is replete with instructive ideas. The beginner must beware of following actual events too closely. There is a danger of accepting actuality instead of literary possibility as the measure of value. *Picturesque*—means fit to be put in a picture, and *literatesque* means fit to be put in a book. In making your plot, therefore, be quite sure you have a subject with these said possibilities in it, and that in developing them by an ordered and cumulative series of events, you are following the wise rule laid down by Aristotle: "Prefer an impossibility which seems probable, to a probability which seems impossible."

Remember always that truth is stranger than fiction. Let facts, newspaper items, things seen and heard, suggest as much as you please, but never follow literally the literal event.

Then your plot must be original. I was amused some time ago by reading the editorial notice to correspondents in an American paper. That editor meant to save the time of his contributors as well as his own, and he gave a list of the plots he did not want. The paper was one which catered for young people. Here is a selection from the list:

1. A lost purse where the finder is tempted to keep it, but finally rises to the emergency and returns it.

2. Heaping coals of fire(!)

3. Saving one's enemy from drowning.

4. Stories of cruel step-mothers.

5. Children praying, and having their prayers answered through being overheard, etc., etc.

Mr Clarence Rook, to whom I have previously referred, says: "There are several plots, four or five, at least. Here are some of the recipes for them. You may rely on them to give thorough satisfaction. Thousands use them daily, and having tried them once, use no other. Take a heroine. The age of heroes is past, and this is the age of heroines. She must be noble, high-souled. (Souls have been worn very high for the past few seasons.) Her soul is too high for conventional morality. Mix her up with some disgraceful situations, taking care to add the purest of motives. Let her poison her mother and run away with a thoughtful scavenger. When you are tired of her you can pitch her over Waterloo Bridge."[6]

Over against this style of criticism I should like to place another which comes from an academic source. Speaking of the plots of Hall Caine's novels, Professor Saintsbury says that, "with the exception of 'The Scapegoat,' there is an extraordinary and almost heroic monotony of plot. One might almost throw Mr Caine's plots into the form which is used by comparative students of folk-lore to tabulate the various versions of the same legends. Two close relations (if not brothers, at least cousins) the relationship being sometimes legal, sometimes only natural, fall in love with the same girl ('Shadow,' 'Hagar,' 'Bondman,' 'Manxman'); in 'The Deemster' the situation is slightly but not really very different, the brother being jealous of the cousin's affection. In almost all cases there is renunciation by one; in all, including 'The Deemster,' one has, if both have not, to pay more or less heavy pen-

---

6. "Hints to Novelists," in *To-Day*, May 8, 1897.

alties for the intended or unintended rivalry. Sometimes, as in 'The Shadow of a Crime,' 'A Son of Hagar,' and 'The Bondman,' filial relations are brought in to augment the strife of sentiment in the individual. Sometimes ('Shadow,' 'Bondman,' and to some extent 'Manxman') the worsted and renouncing party is self-sacrificing more or less all through; sometimes ('Hagar,' 'Deemster,') he is violent for a time, and only at last repents. In two cases ('Deemster,' 'Manxman,') the injured one, or the one who thinks he is injured, has a rival at his mercy in sleep or disease, is tempted to take his life and forbears. This might be worked out still further."[7]

No; you must be original or nothing at all. Of course your originality may not be striking, but, at any rate, make your own plot, and let others judge it. It is far better to do that than to copy others weakly. Originality and sincerity are pretty much the same thing, as Carlyle observed; and if you want a stimulating essay on the subject, read Lewes' "Principles of Success in Literature," a book, by the way, which you ought to master thoroughly.

THE NATURAL HISTORY OF A PLOT

I have quoted already from Wilkie Collins as to the growth of plot from its embryo stages, but that need not deter us from taking an imaginary example. Let us suppose that you have been possessed for some time with the idea of treating the great facts of race and religion as a theme for a novel. After casting about for a suitable illustration, you

---

7. *Fortnightly Review*, vol. lvii. N.S. p. 187.

finally decide that a Jewish girl, with strictly orthodox parentage, shall fall in love with a youth of Gentile blood, and Roman Catholic in religion. That is the bare idea. You can see at once how many dramatic possibilities it presents; for the passion of love in each case is pitted against the forces of religious prejudice; and all the powers of racial exclusiveness are brought into full play. Now, what is the first thing to do? Well, for you as a beginner, it is to decide *how the story shall end*. Why? Because everything depends on that. If you intend them to have a short flirtation, your course of procedure will be very different to that which must inevitably follow if you intend to make them marry. In the first case, you will have to provide for the stern and unalterable facts of race and religion; in the second, for the possibility of their being overcome. To illustrate further, let me suppose that the Jewess and the Gentile youth are ultimately to marry. How will this affect your choice of characters? It will compel you to choose a Jewess who, although brought up in the orthodox fashion, has enough ability and education to appreciate life and thought outside her own immediate circle, and you must invent facts to account for these things, even though she still worships at the synagogue. On the other hand, the Gentile Catholic must be a man of liberal tendencies, or he would never think twice about the Jewess with the possibility of marrying her. He may persuade himself that he is a good Catholic, but you are bound to prepare your readers for actions which, to say the least, are not normal in men of such religious profession.

The choice of your secondary characters is also determined by the end in view. Because your story has to do
with Jews and Catholics, that is no reason why your pages
should be full of Jews and priests. You want just as many
other people, in addition to your hero and heroine, as are
necessary to bring about the *dénouement*: not one more,
not one less. Now, the end in view is to make these young
people triumph over their race and their religion; and over
and above the difficulties they have between themselves,
there are difficulties placed by other people. By whom?
Here is a chance for your inventiveness. I would suggest
as a beginning that you create parents for the girl and for
the man—orthodox in each case, and unyielding to the
last degree. Give them a name, and put them down on
your list. Money is likely to figure in a narrative of this
kind, and you might arrange for the opportune entrance
of an uncle on the girl's side, who threatens to alter his
will (at present made in her interest) if she encourages
the advances of her Gentile lover. On the man's side, the
priest, of course, will have something to say, and you will
be compelled to make a place for him.

In this way your characters will grow to their complete number, and I should advise you to draw up a list of
them, and opposite each one write a few notes describing
the part they will have to play. One word on nomencla-
ture. There is a mystic suitability—at any rate in novels—
between a name and a character. To call your marvellous
heroine "Annie" is to hoist a signal of distress, unless you
have a unique power of characterisation; and to speak
of your hero as "William" is to handicap his movements

from the start. I am not pleading for fancy names, but just for that distinctiveness in choice which the artistic sense decides is fitting.

To return. The end in view will also shape the course of *events*. Instead of arranging that these are to be a series of psychological skirmishes between two people the poles asunder (as would be the case if their relations were superficial), you have to arrange for events where the characters are in dead earnest. Then, too, in order to relieve the tense nature of the narrative, it will be necessary to provide for happenings which, though not exactly humorous, are still light enough to distract the attention from the severer aspects of the story. Further, the natural background should be selected with an eye to the main issue, and each event should have that cumulative effect which ultimately leads the reader on to the climax.

Of course, it is possible to take a quite different *dénouement* to the one here considered. You might make the pair desperately in love, but foiled by some disaster near the end. In this case, as in the other, the narrative will, or ought to, change its perspective accordingly.

SIR WALTER BESANT ON THE EVOLUTION OF A PLOT

In order to illustrate the subject still further, I quote the following:—

"Consider—say, a diamond robbery. Very well: then, first of all, it must be a robbery committed under exceptional and mysterious conditions, otherwise there would be no interest in it. Also, you will perceive that the robbery must be a big and important thing—no little shoplifting business. Next, the person robbed must not be a mere diamond merchant, but a person whose loss will interest the reader, say, one to whom the robbery is all-important. She shall be, say, a vulgar woman with an overweening pride in her jewels, and, of course, without the money to replace them if they are lost. They must be so valuable as to be worn only on extraordinary occasions, and too valuable to be kept at home. They must be consigned to the care of a jeweller who has strong rooms. You observe that the story is now growing. You have got the preliminary germ. How can the strong room be entered and robbed? Well, it cannot. That expedient will not do. Can the diamonds be taken from the lady while she is wearing them? That would have done in the days of the gallant Claude Duval, but it will not do now. Might the house be broken into by a burglar on a night when a lady had worn them and returned? But she would not rest with such a great property in the house unprotected. They must be taken back to their guardian the same night. Thus the only vulnerable point in the care of the diamonds seems their carriage to and from their guardian. They must be stolen between the jeweller's and the owner's house. Then by whom? The robbery must somehow be connected with the hero of the love story—that is indispensable; he must be innocent of all complicity in it—that is equally indispensable; he must preserve our respect; he will have to be somehow a victim: how is that to be managed?

"The story is getting on in earnest. . . . The only way—or the best way—seems, on consideration, to make the lover be the person who is entrusted with the carriage of this precious package of jewels to and from their owner's house. This, however, is not a very distinguishe-dr*ôle* to play; it wants a very skilled hand to interest us in a jeweller's assistant. . . . We must therefore give this young man an exceptional position. Force of circumstances, perhaps, has compelled him to accept the situation which he holds. He need not, again, be a shopman; he may be a confidential *employé*, holding a position of great trust; and he may be a young man with ambitions outside the narrow circle of his work.

"The girl to whom he is engaged must be lovable to begin with; she must be of the same station in life as her lover—that is to say, of the middle class, and preferably of the professional class. As to her home circle, that must be distinctive and interesting."[8]

I need not quote any further for my present purpose, which is to show mental procedure in plot-formation; but the whole article is full of sound teaching on this and other points.

PLOT-FORMATION IN EARNEST

You have now obtained your characters, and a general outline of the events their actions will compass. What comes next? A carefully written-out statement of the story from

---

8.   Besant, "On the Writing of Novels," *Atalanta*, vol i. p. 372.

the beginning to the end; that is the next step. This story should contain just as much as you would give in outlining the plot to a friend in the course of conversation. It would briefly detail the characters and circumstances of the hero and heroine, and the events which led to their first meeting each other. You would then describe the ripening of their friendship, and the gradual growth of social hostility to the idea of a projected union. The psychological transformations, the domestic infelicities, the racial animosities—these will find suitable expression in word and action. At last the season of cruel suspense is over, and the pair have arrived at their great decision. Elaborate preventive plans are arranged to frustrate their purpose, and there is much excitement lest they should succeed; but when all have done their best, the two are happily wedded and the story is ended.

The exercise of writing out a plain, unvarnished statement of what you are going to do is one that will enable you to see whether your story has balance or not, and it will most certainly test its power to interest; for if in its bald form there is real *story* in it, you may well believe that when properly written it will possess the true fascination of fiction.

Now, a plot is much like a drama, and should have a beginning, a middle, and an end; answering roughly to premiss, argument, and conclusion. There is no better training in plot-study than the reading of such a book as Professor Moulton's "Shakespeare as a Dramatic Artist," in which the author, with rare critical skill, exhibits the construction of plots that are an object of never-ceasing wonder. I will dare to reiterate what I have said before. Take your stand at the end of the story, and work it out backwards. For an excellent illustration see Edgar Allan Poe's account of how he came to write "The Raven" (Appendix I). Perhaps you object to this kind of literary dissection? You think it spoils the effect of a work of art to be too familiar with its physiology? I do not grant these points; but even if they are true, that is no reason why you yourself should be offended by the sight of ropes and pulleys behind the scenes. No; work out the details from the end, and not from the beginning. No character and no action should find a place if it contributes nothing towards the *dénouement*.

CHARACTERS FIRST: PLOT AFTERWARDS

It must not be supposed that a plot *always* comes first in the constructing of a novel. Very often the characters suggest themselves long before the story is even vaguely outlined. Nor is there any reason why such a story should be any worse because it did not originate in the usual way. In fact, the probabilities are that it will be all the better, on account of its stress upon character, and the reaction of various characters on each other. I imagine "Jude the Obscure" grew in this fashion. There is no very striking plot in the book; at any rate not the plot we have in mind when we think of "The Moonstone." But if plot means the inevitable evolution of certain men and women in given circumstances, then there is plot of a high order. In the usual acceptation of the term, however, "Jude the

Obscure" is a novel of character; and most probably Jude existed as a creature of imagination months before it was ever thought he would go to Oxford, or have an adventure with Sue. To many men, doubtless, there is far more fascination in conceiving a group of characters in which there are two or three supreme figures, and then setting to work to discover a narrative which will give them the freest action, than in toiling over the bare idea, the subsequent plot, followed by a series of actors and actresses who work out the *dénouement*. Should you belong to this number, do not hesitate to act accordingly. Nothing wooden in style or method finds a place in these pages, and since some of the finest creations have arisen in the order indicated at the head of this section, perhaps you are to be congratulated that the work before you will be a living growth rather than a mechanical contrivance.

THE NATURAL BACKGROUND

Since your story will presumably be located somewhere on this planet, the next thing to do is to obtain a thorough knowledge of the places where your characters will display themselves. If the scenes are laid in a district which you know by heart, you are not likely to go astray; but more often than not, the scenes are largely imaginative, especially in reference to smaller items such as roads, rivers, trees, and woods. The best plan is to follow the example of Thomas Hardy, and draw a map—both geographical and topographical—of the country and the towns in which your hero and heroine, and subordinate characters, will appear for the interest of the reader. That individual does not care to be puzzled with semi-miraculous transmittances through space. I read a novel some time ago, where on one page the heroine was busy shopping in London, and on the next page was—an hour afterwards—quietly having tea with her beloved somewhere in the Midlands. But the drawing of a map, and using it closely, will not merely render such negative assistance as to avoid mistakes of this kind, it will act positively as a stimulus to creative suggestion. You can follow the lover's jealous rival along the road that leads to the meeting-place with increased imaginative power. That measure of realism which makes the ideal both possible and interesting will come all the more easily, because the map aids you in following the movements of your characters; in fact, if you take this second step with serious resolution, it will go far to add that piquant something which renders your story a series of life-like happenings. The result will be equally beneficial to the reader. It may be a moot question as to how far the map in Stevenson's "Treasure Island" deepens the interest of those who read this exciting story, but in my humble opinion it adds an actuality to the events which is most convincing. Mr Maurice Hewlett has followed suit in his "Forest Lovers." I do not say *publish* your map, but *draw* one and use it. A poor story accompanied by a good map would be too ridiculous; so you had better give all your attention to the narrative, and leave the publication of maps until later days.

Chapter IV

Characters and Characterisation

THE CHIEF CHARACTER

In the plot previously outlined, which figure is supreme? It depends. In some senses the supremacy is not a matter of choice, but is decided by the nature of the story. If the man is making the greater sacrifice, it means that, whether you like it or not, his is the struggle that calls for a larger measure of sympathy; and you must assign him the chief place. Still, there are circumstances which would justify a departure from this law—something after the fashion of respecting the rights of a minority. But in our projected narrative, the woman is undoubtedly the supreme character; for the man's battle is mainly one of religious scruple, and only secondarily a question of race; whereas, the Jewess has a vigorous conflict with both race and religion.

Well, what do you know about women? Anything? Do you know how their minds work? how they talk? what they wear? and the thousand and one trivialities that go to make up character portrayal? If you do not know these things, it is a poor look-out for the success of your novel, and you might as well start another story at once. It may be a disputed question as to whether women understand women better than men: the point is, do *you* understand them? Perhaps you know enough for the purposes of a secondary character, but this Jewess is to be supreme; you must know enough to meet the highest demands.

Where to obtain this knowledge? Ah! Where! Only by studying human lives, human manners, human weaknesses—everything human. The life of the world must become your text-book; as for temperaments, you should know them by heart; social influences in their effect on action and outlook, ought to be within easy comprehension; and even then, you will still cry "Mystery!"

HOW TO PORTRAY CHARACTER

The first thing is to *realise* your characters—*i.e.* make them real persons to yourself, and then you will be more likely to persuade the reader that they are real people. Unless this is done, your hero and heroine will be described as "puppets" or "abstractions." I am not saying the task is easy—in fact, it is one of the most difficult that the novelist has to face. But there is no profit in shirking it, and the sooner it is dealt with the better. The history of character representation in drama is full of luminous teaching, and a study of it cannot be other than highly instructive. In the early *Mystery* and *Morality* plays, virtues and vices were each apportioned their respective actors—that is to say, one man set forth Good Counsel, another Repentance, another Gluttony, and another Pride. Even so late as Philip Massinger's "A New Way to Pay Old Debts," we have Wellborn, Justice, Greedy, Tapwell, Froth, and Furnace. Now this seems very elementary to us, but it has one great merit: the audience knew what each character stood for, and could form an intelligent idea of his place in the piece. In these days we have become more subtle—necessarily so. Following the lead of the Shakespearean dramatists, we have not described our characters by giving them names—virtuous or otherwise—we let them describe themselves by their speech and action. The essential thing is that we should know our characters intimately, so intimately that, although they exist in imagination alone, they are as real to us as the members of our own family. Falstaff never had flesh and blood, but as Shakespeare portrayed him, you feel that you have only to prick him and he will bleed. The historical Hamlet is a mist; the Hamlet of the play is a reality.

This power of realisation depends on two things: *Observation with insight, and Sympathy with imagination.* Observation is a most valuable gift, but without insight it is likely to work mischief by creating a tendency to write down just what you see and hear. Zola's novels too often suggest the note-book. Avoid photographing life as you would avoid a dangerous foe. The newspaper reporter can "beat you hollow," for that is his special subject: life as it is. Observe what goes on around you, but get behind the scenes; study selfishness and "otherness," and the inter-play of motives, the conflict of interests which causes this tangle of human affairs—in other words, obtain an insight into them by asking the "why" and "wherefore."

Above all, learn to see with other people's eyes, and to feel with other people's hearts. For instance, you may find it needful to attend synagogue-worship in order to obtain a first-hand knowledge of the religion of your Jewish heroine. When you see the men in silk hats, and praying-shawls over their shoulders, you may be tempted to despise Judaism; the result being that you determine not to cumber your novel with a description of such "nonsense." Well, you will lose one of the most picturesque features of your story; you will fail to see the part which the synagogue plays in your heroine's mental struggle, and the portrayal of her character will be sadly defective in consequence. No; a novelist, as such, should have no religion, no politics, no social creed; whatever he believes as a private individual should not interfere with the outgoing of sympathy in constructing the characters he intends to set forth. Human nature is a compound of the virtuous and the vicious, or, to change the figure, a perpetual oscillation between flesh and spirit. Life is half tragedy and half comedy: men and women are sometimes wise and often foolish. From this maze of mystery you are to develop new creations, and actual people are your *starting-point*, never your *models*.

METHODS OF CHARACTERISATION

By characterisation is meant the power to make your ideal persons appear real. It is one thing to make them real to yourself, and quite another thing to make them real to other people. Characterisation needs a union of imaginative and artistic gifts. In this respect, as in all others,

Shakespeare is pre-eminent. His characters are alike clear in conception and expression, and their human quality is just as wonderful as the large scale on which they move, covering, as they do, the entire field of human nature.

There are certain well-known methods of character-isation, and to these I propose to devote the remainder of this chapter. The first and most obvious is for the author to describe the character. This is generally recognised as bad art. To say "She was a very wicked woman," is like the boy who drew a four-legged animal and wrote underneath, "This is a cow." If that boy had succeeded in drawing a cow there would have been no need to label it; and, in the same way, if you succeed in realising and drawing your characters there will be no need to talk about them. The best characterisation never *says* what a person is; it shows what he or she is by what they do and say. I do not mean that you must say nothing at all about your creations; the novels of Hardy and Meredith contain a good deal of indirect comment of this kind; but it is a notable fact that Hardy's weakest work, "A Laodicean," contains more comment than any of the others he has written. Stevenson aptly said, "Readers cannot fail to have remarked that what an author tells us of the beauty or the charm of his creatures goes for nought; that we know instantly better; that the heroine cannot open her mouth but what, all in a moment, the fine phrases of preparation fall from her like the robes of Cinderella, and she stands before us as a poor, ugly, sickly wench, or perhaps a strapping market-woman."

There is another point to be remembered. If you label a character at the outset as a very humorous person, the reader prepares himself for a good laugh now and then, and if you disappoint him—well, you have lost a reader and gained an adverse critic. To announce beforehand what you are going to do, and then fail, is to put a weapon into the hands of those who honour you with a reading. "Often a single significant detail will throw more light on a character than pages of comment. An example in perfection is the phrase in which Thackeray tells how Becky Crawley, amid all her guilt and terror, when her husband had Lord Steyne by the throat, felt a sudden thrill of admiration for Rawdon's splendid strength. It is like a flash of lightning which shows the deeps of the selfish, sensual woman's nature. It is no wonder that Thackeray threw down his pen, as he confessed that he did, and cried, 'That is a stroke of genius.'"

The lesson is plain. Don't say what your hero and heroine *are*: make them tell their own characters by words and deeds.

THE TRICK OF "IDIOSYNCRASIES"

Young writers, who fail to mark off the individuality of one character from another, by the strong lines of difference which are found in real life, endeavour to atone for their incompetency by emphasising physical and mental oddities. This is a mere literary "trick." To invest your hero with a squint, or an irritating habit of blowing his nose continually; or to make your heroine guilty of using a few funny phrases every time she speaks, is certainly to distinguish them from the other characters in the book who cannot boast of such excellences, but it must not be called characterisation. It is a bastard attempt to econo- mise the labour that is necessary to discover individuality of soul and to bring it out in skilful dialogues and care- fully chosen situations.

Another form of the trick of idiosyncrasy is the bald realism of the sensationalist. He persuades himself that he is character-drawing. He is doing nothing of the kind. He takes snap-shots with a literary camera and reproduces direct from the negative. The art of re-touching nature so that it becomes ideal, is not in his line at all: the com- mercial instinct in him is stronger than the artistic, and he sees more business in realism than in idealism. And what is more, there is less labour—characters exist ready for use. It is easy to listen to a lively altercation between cabbies in a London street, when language passes that makes one hesitate to strike a match, and then go home and draw a city driver. You have no need to search for contrasts, for colour, for sound, for passion: you saw and heard everything at once. But the truth still remains— the seeing of things, and the hearing of things, are but the raw material: where are your new creations?

The trick of selecting oddities as a method of char- acterisation is superficial, simply because oddities lie upon the surface. You can, without much difficulty, construct a dialogue between a blacksmith and a student, showing how the unlettered man exhibits his ignorance and the scholar his taste. But such a distinction is quite external; at heart the men may be very much alike. It is one thing to paint the type, and another to paint the individual. Take Sir Willoughby Patterne. He is a man who belongs to the type "selfish"; but he is much more than a typically selfish man; he is an *individual*. There is a turn in his remarks, a way of speaking in dialogue, and a style of doing things which show him to be self-centred, not in a general way, but in the particular way of Sir Willoughby Patterne.

There is one fact in characterisation for which a due margin should always be made. Wilkie Collins, you will remember, says of his Fosco: "The making him fat was an afterthought; his canaries and his white mice were found next; and the most valuable discovery of all, his admiration of Miss Halcombe, took its rise in a conviction that he would not be true to nature unless there was some weak point somewhere in his character." You must provide for these "afterthoughts" by not being too ready to cast your characters in the final mould. Let every personality be in a state of *becoming* until he has actually *come*—in all the completeness of appearance, manner, speech, and action. Your first conception of the Jewess may be that of one who possesses the usual physique of her class—short and stout; but afterwards it may suit your purpose better to make her fairer, taller, and slighter, than the rest of her race. If so, do not hesitate to undo the work of laborious hours by effecting such an improvement. It will go against the grain, no doubt; but novel-writing is a serious business, and much depends on trifles in accomplishing success; so do not begrudge the extra toil involved.

Characterisation is the finest feature of the novelist's art. Here you will have your greatest difficulties, but, if you overcome them, you will have your greatest triumphs. Here, too, the crying need is a knowledge of human nature. Acquire a mastership of this subtle quantity, and then you may hope for genuine results. Of course, knowledge is not *all*; it is in artistic appreciation that true character-drawing consists.

Chapter V

Studies in Literary Technique

NARRATIVE ART

David Pryde has summed up the whole matter in a few well-chosen sentences: "Keeping the beginning and the end in view, we set out from the right starting-place, and go straight towards the destination; we introduce no event that does not spring from the first cause and tend to the great effect; we make each detail a link joined to the one going before and the one coming after; we make, in fact, all the details into one entire chain, which we can take up as a whole, carry about with us, and retain as long as we please."[9] How many elements are here referred to? There are plot, movement, unity, proportion, purpose, and climax. I have already dealt with some of these, and now propose to devote a few paragraphs to the rest.

Unity means unity of effect, and is first a matter of literary architecture—afterwards a matter of impression. It has been said of Macbeth that "the play moves forward with an absolute regularity; it is almost architectural in its rise and fall, in the balance of its parts. The plot is a complex one; it has an ebb and flow, a complication

---

9. "Studies in Composition," p. 26.

and a resolution, to use technical terms. That is to say, the fortunes of Macbeth swoop up to a crisis or turning-point, and thence down again to a catastrophe. The catastrophe, of course, closes the play; the crisis, as so often with Shakespeare, comes in its exact centre, in the middle of the middle act, with the Escape of Fleance. Hitherto Macbeth's path has been gilded with success; now the epoch of failure begins. And the parallelisms and correspondences throughout are remarkable. Each act has a definite subject: The Temptation; The First, Second, and Third Crimes; The Retribution. Three accidents, if we may so call them, help Macbeth in the first part of the play: the visit of Duncan to Inverness, his own impulsive murder of the grooms, the flight of Malcolm and Donalbain. And in the second half three accidents help to bring about his ruin: the escape of Fleance, the false prophecy of the witches, the escape of Macduff. Malcolm and Macduff at the end answer to Duncan and Banquo at the beginning. A meeting with the witches heralds both rise and fall. Finally, each of the crimes is represented in the Retribution. Malcolm, the son of Duncan, and Macduff, whose wife and child he slew, conquer Macbeth; Fleance begets a race that shall reign in his stead."[10]

From a construction point of view, a novel and a play have many points in common; and although the parallelism of events and characters is not necessary for either, the account of Macbeth just given is a good illustration of unity of effect and impression. Stevenson's "Kidnapped" and "David Balfour" are good examples of unity of structure.

---

10. E. K. Chambers' *Macbeth*, pp. 25, 26. "The Warwick Shakespeare."

MOVEMENT

How many times have you put a novel away with the remark: "It *drags* awfully!" The narrative that drags is not worthy of the name. There are a few writers who can go into byways and take the reader with them—Mr Le Gallienne, for instance—but, as a rule, the digressive novelist is the one whose book is thrown on to the table with the remark just quoted. A story should be *progressive*, not *digressive* and episodical. Hence the importance of movement and suspense. Keep your narrative in motion, and do not let it sleep for a while unless it is of deliberate intention. There is a definite law to be observed—namely, that as feeling rises higher, sentences become crisp and shorter; witness Acts i. and ii. in *Macbeth*. Suspense, too, is an agent in accelerating the forward march of a story. There is no music in a pause, but it renders great service in giving proper emphasis to music that goes before and comes after it. Notice how Stevenson employs suspense and contrast in "Kidnapped." "The sea had gone down, and the wind was steady and kept the sails quiet, so that there was a great stillness in the ship, in which I made sure I heard the sound of muttering voices. A little after, and there came a clash of steel upon the deck, by which I knew they were dealing out the cutlasses, and one had been let fall; and after that silence again." These little touches are capable of affecting the entire interest of the whole story, and should receive careful attention.

AIDS TO DESCRIPTION: THE POINT OF VIEW

So much has been said in praise of descriptive power, that it will not be amiss if I repeat one or two opinions which, seemingly, point the other way. Gray, in a letter to West, speaks of describing as "an ill habit that will wear off"; and Disraeli said description was "always a bore both to the describer and the describee." To some, these authorities may not be of sufficient weight. Will they listen to Robert Louis Stevenson? He says that "no human being ever spoke of scenery for above two minutes at a time, which makes one suspect we hear too much of it in literature." These remarks will save us from that description-worship which is a sort of literary influenza.

The first thing to be determined in descriptive art is *the point of view*. Suppose you are standing on an eminence commanding a wide stretch of plain with a river winding through it. What does the river look like? A silver thread; and so you would describe it. But if you stood close to the brink and looked back to the eminence on which you stood previously, you would no longer speak of a silver thread, simply because now your point of view is changed. The principle is elementary enough, and there is no need to dwell upon it further, except to quote an illustration from Blackmore:

"For she stood at the head of a deep green valley, carved from out the mountains in a perfect oval, with a fence of sheer rock standing round it, eighty feet or a hundred high, from whose brink black wooded hills swept up to the skyline. By her side a little river glided out from underground with a soft, dark babble, unawares of daylight; then growing brighter, lapsed away, and fell into the valley. Then, as it ran down the meadow, alders stood on either marge, and grass was blading out of it, and yellow tufts of rushes gathered, looking at the hurry. But further down, on either bank, were covered houses built of stone, square, and roughly covered, set as if the brook were meant to be the street between them. Only one room high they were, and not placed opposite each other, but in and out as skittles are; only that the first of all, which proved to be the captain's was a sort of double house, or rather two houses joined together by a plank-bridge over the river."[11]

SELECTING THE MAIN FEATURES

The fundamental principle of all art is selection, and nowhere is it seen to better advantage than in description. A battle, a landscape, or a mental agony, can only be described artistically, in so far as the writer chooses the most characteristic features for presentation. In the following passage George Eliot states the law and keeps it. "She had time to remark that he was a peculiar-looking person, but not insignificant, which was the quality that most hopelessly consigned a man to perdition. He was massively built. The striking points in his face were large, clear, grey eyes, and full lips." Suppose for a moment that the reader were told about the pattern and "hang" of the hero's trousers, his waistcoat and his coat, and that information was given respecting the number of links in his watch-chain,

---

11. "Lorna Doone."

and the exact depth of his double chin—what would have been the effect from an artistic point of view? Failure—for instead of getting a description alive with interest, we should get a catalogue wearisome in its multiplicity of detail. A certain author once thought Homer was niggardly in describing Helen's charms, so he endeavoured to atone for the great poet's shortcomings in the following manner:—"She was a woman right beautiful, with fine eyebrows, of clearest complexion, beautiful cheeks; comely, with large, full eyes, with snow-white skin, quick glancing, graceful; a grove filled with graces, fair-armed, voluptuous, breathing beauty undisguised. The complexion fair, the cheek rosy, the countenance pleasing, the eye blooming, a beauty unartificial, untinted, of its natural colour, adding brightness to the brightest cherry, as if one should dye ivory with resplendent purple. Her neck long, of dazzling whiteness, whence she was called the swan-born, beautiful Helen."

After reading this can you form a distinct idea of Helen's beauty? We think not. The details are too many, the language too exuberant, and the whole too much in the form of a catalogue. It would have been better to select a few of what George Eliot calls the "striking points," and present them with taste and skill. As it is, the attempt to improve on Homer has resulted in a description which, for detail and minuteness, is like the enumeration of the parts of a new motor-car—indeed, that is the true sphere of description by detail, where, as in all matters mechanical, fulness and accuracy are demanded. In "Mariana,"

Tennyson refers to no more facts than are necessary to emphasise her great loneliness:

"With blackest moss the flower-potsWere thickly crusted, one and all;The rusted nails fell from the knotsThat held the pear to the gable wall.The broken sheds looked sad and strange:Unlifted was the clinking latch;Weeded and worn the ancient thatchUpon the lonely moated grange."

In ordering such details as may be chosen to represent an event, idea, or person, it is the rule to proceed from "the near to the remote, and from the obvious to the obscure." Homer thus describes a shield as smooth, beautiful, brazen, and well-hammered—that is, he gives the particulars in the order in which they would naturally be observed. Homer's method is also one of epithet: "the far-darting Apollo," "swift-footed Achilles," "wide-ruling Agamemnon," "white-armed Hera," and "bright-eyed Athene." Now it is but a step from this giving of epithets to what is called

DESCRIPTION BY SUGGESTION

When Hawthorne speaks of the "black, moody brow of Septimus Felton," it is really suggestion by the use of epithet. Dickens took the trouble to enumerate the characteristics of Mrs Gamp one by one; but he succeeded in presenting Mrs Fezziwig by simply saying, "In came Mrs Fezziwig, one vast substantial smile." This latter method differs from the former in almost every possible way. The enumeration of details becomes wearisome unless very cleverly handled, whereas the suggestive method unifies the writer's impressions, thereby saving the reader's mental exertions and heightening his pleasures. He tells us how things and persons impress him, and prefers to *indicate* rather than describe. Thus Dickens refers to "a full-sized, sleek, well-conditioned gentleman in a blue coat with bright buttons, and a white cravat. This gentleman had a very red face, as if an undue proportion of the blood in his body had been squeezed into his head; which perhaps accounted for his having also the appearance of being rather cold about the heart." Lowell says of Chaucer, "Sometimes he describes amply by the merest hint, as where the Friar, before sitting himself down, drives away the cat. We know without need of more words that he has chosen the snuggest corner."

Notice how succinctly Blackmore delineates a natural fact, "And so in a sorry plight I came to an opening in the bushes where a great black pool lay in front of me, whitened with snow (as I thought) at the sides, till I saw it was only foam-froth, . . . and the look of this black pit was enough to stop one from diving into it, even on a hot summer's day, with sunshine on the water; I mean if the sun ever shone there. As it was, I shuddered and drew back; not alone at the pool itself, and the black air there was about it, but also at the whirling manner, and wisping of white threads upon it in stripy circles round and round; and the centre still as jet."[12]

Hardy's description of Egdon Heath is too well known to need remark; it is a classic of its kind.

---

12. "Lorna Doone."

Robert Louis Stevenson possessed the power of suggestion to a high degree. "An ivory-faced and silver-haired old woman opened the door. She had an evil face, smoothed with hypocrisy, but her manners were excellent." To advise a young writer to imitate Stevenson would be absurd, but perhaps I may be permitted to say: study Stevenson's method, from the blind man in "Treasure Island," to Kirstie in "The Weir of Hermiston."

FACTS TO REMEMBER

"It is a peculiarity of Walter Scott," says Goethe, "that his great talent in representing details often leads him into faults. Thus in 'Ivanhoe' there is a scene where they are seated at a table in a castle-hall, at night, and a stranger enters. Now he is quite right in describing the stranger's appearance and dress, but it is a fault that he goes to the length of describing his feet, shoes and stockings. When we sit down in the evening and someone comes in, we notice only the upper part of his body. If I describe the feet, daylight enters at once and the scene loses its nocturnal character." And yet Scott in some respects was a master of description—witness his picture of Norham Castle and of the ravine of Greeta between Rokeby and Mortham. But Goethe's criticism is justified notwithstanding. Never write more than can be said of a man or a scene when regarded from the surrounding circumstances of light and being. Ruskin is never tired of saying, "Draw what you see." In the "Fighting Téméraire," Turner paints the old warship as if it had no rigging. It was there in its proper place, but the artist could not see it, and he refused to put it in his picture if, at the distance, it was not visible. "When you see birds fly, you do not see any *feathers*," says Mr W. M. Hunt. "You are not to draw *reality*, but reality as it *appears* to you."

Avoid the *pathetic fallacy*. Kingsley, in "Alton Locke," says:

"They rowed her in across the rolling foam—The cruel crawling foam,"

on which Ruskin remarks, "The foam is not cruel, neither does it crawl. The state of mind which attributes to it these characteristics of a living creature is one in which the reason is unhinged by grief. All violent feelings have the same effect. They produce in us a falseness in all our impressions of external things."

Perhaps the secret of all accurate description is a trained eye. Do you know how a cab-driver mounts on to the box, or the shape of a coal-heaver's mouth when he cries "Coal!"? Do you know how a wood looks in early spring as distinct from its precise appearance in summer, or how a man uses his eyes when concealing feelings of jealousy? or a woman when hiding feelings of love? Observation with insight, and Imagination with sympathy; these are the great necessities in every department of novel-writing.

Chapter VI

Studies in Literary Technique

COLOUR: LOCAL AND OTHERWISE

One morning you opened your paper and found that Mr Simon St Clair had gone into Wales in search of local colour. What does local colour mean? The appearance of the country, the dress and language of the people, all that distinguishes the particular locality from others near and remote—is local colour. Take Kipling's "Mandalay" as an illustration. He speaks of the ringing temple bell, of the garlic smells, and the dawn that comes up like thunder; there are elephants piling teak, and all the special details of the particular locality find a characteristic expression. For what reason? Well, local colour renders two services to literature; it makes very often a pleasing or a striking picture in itself; and it is used by the author to bring out special features in his story. Kipling's underlying idea comes to the surface when he says that a man who has lived in the East always hears the East "a-callin'" him back again. There is deep pathos in the idea alone; but when it is set in the external characteristics of Eastern life, one locality chosen to set forth the rest, and stated in language that few can equal, the entire effect is very striking.

Whenever local colour is of picturesque quality there is a temptation to substitute "word-painting" for the story. The desire for novelty is at the bottom of a good deal of modern extravagance in this direction, but the truth still remains that local colour has an important function to discharge—namely, to increase the artistic value of good narrative by suggesting the environment of the *dramatis personæ*. You must have noticed the opening chapters of "The Scarlet Letter." Why all this careful detailing of the Customs House, the manners and the talk of the people? For no other reason than that just given.

But there is another use of colour in literary composition. Perhaps I can best illustrate my purpose by quoting from an interview with James Lane Allen, who certainly ought to know what he is talking about. The author of "The Choir Invisible," and "Summer in Arcady," occupies a position in Fiction which makes his words worth considering.

Said Mr Allen to the interviewer:[13] "A friend of mine—a painter—had just finished reading some little thing that I had succeeded in having published in the *Century*. 'What do you think of it?' I asked him. 'Tell me frankly what you like and what you don't like.'

"'It's interestingly told, dramatic, polished, and all that, Allen,' was his reply, 'but why in the world did you neglect such an opportunity to drop in some colour here, and at this point, and there?'

---

13. Shuman, "Steps into Journalism," p. 201.

"It came over me like that," said the Kentuckian, snapping his fingers, "that words indicating colours can be manipulated by the writer just as pigments are by the painter. I never forgot the lesson. And now when I describe a landscape, or a house, or a costume, I try to put it into such words that an artist can paint the scene from my words."

Evidently Mr Allen learned his lesson long ago, but it is one every writer should study carefully. Mr Baring Gould also gives his experience. "In one of my stories I sketched a girl in a white frock leaning against a sunny garden wall, tossing guelder-roses. I had some burnished gold-green flies on the old wall, preening in the sun; so, to complete the scene, I put her on gold-green leather shoes, and made the girl's eyes of much the same hue. Thus we had a picture where the colour was carried through, and, if painted, would have been artistic and satisfying. A red sash would have spoiled all, so I gave her one that was green. So we had the white dress, the guelder-rose-balls greeny-white, and through the ranges of green-gold were led up to her hair, which was red-gold. I lay some stress on this formation of picture in tones of colour, because it pleases myself when writing—it satisfies my artistic sense. A thousand readers may not observe it; but those who have any art in them will at once receive therefrom a pleasing impression."[14]

These two testimonies make the matter very plain. If anything is needed it is a more practical illustration tak-

---

14. "The Art of Writing Fiction," p. 40.

en direct from a book. For this purpose I have chosen a choice piece from George Du Maurier's "Peter Ibbetson," a book that was half-killed by the Trilby boom.

"Before us lies a sea of fern, gone a russet-brown from decay, in which are isles of dark green gorse, and little trees with scarlet and orange and lemon-coloured leaflets fluttering down, and running after each other on the bright grass, under the brisk west wind which makes the willows rustle, and turn up the whites of their leaves in pious resignation to the coming change.

"Harrow-on-the-Hill, with its pointed spire, rises blue in the distance; and distant ridges, like the receding waves, rise into blueness, one after the other, out of the low-lying mist; the last ridge bluely melting into space. In the midst of it all, gleams the Welsh Harp Lake, like a piece of sky that has become unstuck and tumbled into the landscape with its shiny side up."

WHAT ABOUT DIALECT?

Dialect is local colour individualised. Ian Maclaren, in "The Bonnie Brier Bush," following in the wake of Crockett and Barrie, has given us the dialect of Scotland: Baring Gould and a host of others have provided us with dialect stories of English counties; Jane Barlow and several Irish writers deal with the sister island; Wales has not been forgotten; and the American novelists have their big territory mapped out into convenient sections. Soon the acreage of locality literature will have been completely "written up"; I do not say its yielding powers will have been exhausted, for, as with other species of local colour, dialect has had to suffer at the hands of the imitator who dragged dialect into his paltry narrative for its own sake, and to give him the opportunity of providing the reader with a glossary.

The reason why dialect-stories were so popular some time ago is twofold. First, dialect imparts a flavour to a narrative, especially when it is in contrast to educated utterances on the part of other characters. But the chief reason is that dialect people have more character than other people—as a rule. They afford greater scope for literary artistry than can be found in life a stage or two higher, with its correctness and artificiality. St Beuve said, "All peasants have style." Yes; that is the truth exactly. There is an individuality about the peasant that is absent from the town-dweller, and this fact explains the piquancy of many novels that owe their popularity to the representations of the rustic population. The dialect story, or novel, cannot hope for permanency unless it contains elements of universal interest. The emphasis laid on a certain type of speech stamps such a literary production with the brand of narrowness. I understand that Ian Maclaren has been translated into French. Can you imagine Drumsheugh in Gallic? or Jamie Soutar? Never. Only that which is literature in the highest sense can be translated into another language; hence the life of corners in Scotland, or elsewhere, has no special interest for the world in general.

The rule as to dealing with dialect is quite simple. Never use the letters of the alphabet to reproduce the sound of such language in a literal manner. *Suggest dialect*; that is all. Have nothing to do with glossaries. People hate dictionaries, however brief, when they read fiction. George Eliot and Thomas Hardy are good models of the wise use of county speech.

ON DIALOGUE

In making your characters talk, it should be your aim not to *reproduce* their conversation, but to *indicate* it. Here, as elsewhere, the first principle of all art is selection, and from the many words which you have heard your characters use, you must choose those that are typical in view of the purpose you have in hand. I once had a letter from a youthful novelist, in which he said: "It's splendid to write a story. I make my characters say what I like—swear, if necessary—and all that." Now you can't make your characters say what you like; you are obliged to make them say what is in keeping with their known dispositions, and with the circumstances in which they are placed at the time of speaking. If you know your characters intimately, you will not put wise words into the mouth of a clown, unless you have suitably provided for such a surprise; neither will you write long speeches for the sullen villain who is to be the human devil of the narrative. Remember, therefore, that the key to propriety and effectiveness in writing is the knowledge of those ideal people whom you are going to use in your pages.

"Windiness" and irrelevancy are the twin evils of conversations in fiction. Trollope says, "It is so easy to make two persons talk on any casual subject with which the writer presumes himself to be conversant! Literature, philosophy, politics, or sport may be handled in a loosely discursive style; and the writer, while indulging himself, is apt to think he is pleasing the reader. I think he can make no greater mistake. The dialogue is generally the most agreeable part of a novel; but it is only so as long as it tends in some way to the telling of the main story. It need not be confined to this, but it should always have a tendency in that direction. The unconscious critical acumen of a reader is both just and severe. When a long dialogue on extraneous matter reaches his mind, he at once feels that he is being cheated into taking something that he did not bargain to accept when he took up the novel. He does not at that moment require politics or philosophy, but he wants a story. He will not, perhaps, be able to say in so many words that at some point the dialogue has deviated from the story; but when it does, he will feel it."[15]

A word or two as to what kind of dialogue assists in telling the main story may not be amiss. Return to the suggested plot of the Jewess and the Roman Catholic. What are they to talk about? Anything that will assist their growing intimacy, that will bring out the peculiar personalities of both, and contribute to the development of the narrative. In a previous section I said that the *dénouement* decided the selection of your characters; in some respects it will also decide the topics of their conversation. Certain events have to be provided for, in order that they

---

15. "Autobiography," vol. ii. p. 58.

may be both natural and inevitable, and it becomes your duty to create incidents and introduce dialogue which will lead up to these events.

With reference to models for study, advice is difficult to give. Quite a gallery of masters would be needed for the purpose, as there are so many points in one which are lacking in another. Besides, a great novelist may have eccentricities in dialogue, and be quite normal in other respects. George Meredith is as artificial in dialogue as he is in the use of phrases pure and simple, and yet he succeeds, *in spite of* defects, not *by* them. Here is a sample from "The Egoist":

"Have you walked far to-day?"

"Nine and a half hours. My Flibbertigibbet is too much for me at times, and I had to walk off my temper."

"All those hours were required?"

"Not quite so long."

"You are training for your Alpine tour?"

"It's doubtful whether I shall get to the Alps this year. I leave the Hall, and shall probably be in London with a pen to sell."

"Willoughby knows that you leave him?"

"As much as Mont Blanc knows that he is going to be climbed by a party below. He sees a speck or two in the valley."

"He has spoken of it."

"He would attribute it to changes."

I need not discuss how far this advances the novelist's narrative, but it is plain that it is not a model for the beginner. For smartness and "point" nothing could be better than Anthony Hope's "Dolly Dialogues," although the style is not necessarily that of a novel.

POINTS IN CONVERSATION

Never allow the reader to be in doubt as to who is speaking. When he has to turn back to discover the speaker's identity, you may be sure there is something wrong with your construction. You need not quote the speaker's name in order to make it plain that he is speaking: all that is needed is a little attention to the "said James" and "replied Susan" of your dialogues. When once these two have commenced to talk, they can go on in catechism form for a considerable period. But if a third party chimes in, a more careful disposition of names is called for.

Beginners very often have a good deal of trouble with their "saids," "replieds," and "answereds."

Here, again, a little skilful manœvring will obviate the difficulty. This is a specimen of third-class style.

"I'm off on Monday," *said* he.

"Not really," *said* she.

"Yes, I have only come to say goodbye," *said* he.

"Shall you be gone long?" *asked* she.

"That depends," *said* he.

"I should like to know what takes you away," *said* she.

"I daresay," *said* he, smiling.

"I shouldn't wonder if I know," *said* she.

"I daresay you might guess," *said* he.

Could anything be more wooden than this perpetual "said he, said she," which I have accentuated by putting into italics? Now, observe the difference when you read the following:—

Observed Silver.

Cried the Cook.

Returned Morgan.

Said Another.

Agreed Silver.

Said the fellow with the bandage.

There is no lack of suitable verbs for dialogue purposes—remarked, retorted, inquired, demanded, murmured, grumbled, growled, sneered, explained, and a host more. Without a ready command of such a vocabulary you cannot hope to give variety to your character-conversations, and, what is of graver importance, you will not be able to bring out the essential qualities of such remarks as you introduce. For instance, to put a sarcastic utterance into a man's mouth, and then to write down that he "replied" with those words is not half so effective as to say he "sneered" them.[16]

Probably you will be tempted to comment on your dialogue as you write by insinuating remarks as to actions, looks, gestures, and the like. This is a good temptation, so far, but it has its dangers. The ancient Hebrew writer, in telling the story of Hezekiah, said that Isaiah went to the king with these words:

"Set thine house in order: for thou shalt die and not live."

And Hezekiah turned his face to the wall—and prayed.

If you can make a comment as dramatic and forceful as that, *make it.* But avoid useless and uncalled-for remarks, and remember that you really want nothing, not even a fine epigram, which fails to contribute to the main purpose.

"ATMOSPHERE"

It will not be inappropriate to close this chapter with a few words on what is called "atmosphere." The word is often met with in the vocabulary of the reviewer; he is marvellously keen in scenting atmospheres. Perhaps an illustration may be the best means of exposition. The reviewer is speaking of Maeterlinck's "Alladine and Palomides," "Interior," and "The Death of Tintagiles." He says, "We

---

16. See Bates' "Talks on Writing English." An excellent manual, to which I am indebted for ideas and suggestions.

find in them the same strange atmosphere to which we had grown accustomed in 'Pelleas' and 'L'Intruse.' We are in a region of no fixed plane—a region that this world never saw. It is a region such as Arnold Böcklin, perhaps, might paint, and many a child describe. A castle stands upon a cliff. Endless galleries and corridors and winding stairs run through it. Beneath lie vast grottoes where subterranean waters throw up unearthly light from depths where seaweed grows." This is very true, and put into bald language it means that Maeterlinck has succeeded in creating an artistic environment for his weird characters; it is the*setting* in which he has placed them. In the first scene of *Hamlet*, Shakespeare creates the necessary atmosphere to introduce the events that are to follow. The soldiers on guard are concerned and afraid; the reader is thereby prepared, step by step, for the reception of the whole situation; everything that will strengthen the impression of a coming fatality is seized by a master hand, and made to do service in creating an atmosphere of such expectant quality. An artist by nature will select intuitively the persons and facts he needs; but there is no reason why a study of these necessities, a slow and careful pondering, should not at last succeed in alighting upon the precise and inevitable details which delicately and subtly produce the desired result. In this sense the matter can hardly be called a minor detail, but the expression has been sufficiently guarded.

Chapter VII

Pitfalls

ITEMS OF GENERAL KNOWLEDGE

I propose to show in this chapter that a literary artist can never afford to despise details. He may have genius enough to write a first-rate novel, and sell it rapidly in spite of real blemishes, but if a work of art is worth doing at all, it is worth doing well. No writer is any the better for slovenly inaccuracy. Take the details of everyday life. Do you suppose you are infallible in these commonplace things? If so, be undeceived at once. It is simply marvellous with what ease a mistake will creep into your narrative. Even Mr Zangwill once made a hansom cab door to open with a handle from the inside, and the mistake appeared in six editions, escaping the reviewers, and was quietly altered by the author in the seventh. There is nothing particularly serious about an error of this kind; but at the same time, where truth to fact is so simple a matter, why not give the fact as it is? Trivialities may not interfere with the power of the story, but they often attach an ugliness, or a smack of the ridiculous, which cannot but hinder, to some extent, the beauty of otherwise good work. Mistakes such as that just referred to, arise, in most instances, out of the passion and feeling in which the novelist advances his narrative. The detail connected with the opening of the hansom door (doors) was nothing to Mr Zangwill, compared to the person who opened it. I should advise you, therefore, to master all the necessary *minutiae* of travelling, if your hero and heroine are going abroad; of city life if you take them to the theatre for amusement—in fact, of every environment in which imagination may place them. Then, when all your work is done, read what has been written with the microscopic eyes of a Flaubert.

SPECIFIC SUBJECTS

For instance, the plot suggested in the previous chapters deals with Judaism. Now, if you don't know Jewish life through and through, it is the height of foolishness to attempt to write a novel about it. (The same remark applies to Roman Catholicism.) You will find it necessary to study the Bible and Hebrew history; and when you have mastered the literature of the subject and caught its spirit, you will turn your attention to the sacred people as they exist to-day—their isolation, their wealth, their synagogues, and their psychological peculiarities. Does this seem to be too big a programme? Well, if you are to present a living and truthful picture of the Jewess and her surroundings, you can only succeed by going through such a programme; whereas, if you skip the hard preparatory work you will bungle in the use of Hebrew terms, and when you make the Rabbi drop the scroll through absent-mindedness, you will very likely say that "the congregation looked on half-amused and half-wondering."

Just visit a synagogue when the Rabbi happens to drop the scroll. The congregation would be "horribly shocked." The same law applies whatever be your subject. If you intend to follow a prevailing fashion and depict slum life, you will have to spend a good deal of time in those unpleasant regions, not only to know them in their outward aspects, but to know them in their inward and human features. Even then something important may escape you, with the result that you fall into error, and the expert enjoys a quiet giggle at your expense; but you will have some consolation in the thought that you spared no pains in the diligent work of preparation.

Perhaps your novel will take the reader into aristocratic circles. Pray do not make the attempt if you are not thoroughly acquainted with the manners and customs of such circles. Ignorance will surely betray you, and in describing a dinner, or an "At Home," you will raise derisive laughter by suggesting the details of a most impossible meal, or spoil your heroine by making her guilty of atrocious etiquette. The remedy is close at hand: *know your subject.*

TOPOGRAPHY AND GEOGRAPHY

Watch your topography and geography. Have you never read novels where the characters are made to walk miles of country in as many minutes? In fairy tales we rather like these extraordinary creatures—their startling performances have a charm we should be sorry to part with. But in the higher world of fiction, where ideal things should appear as real as possible, we decidedly object to miraculous journeys, especially, as in most instances, it is plainly a mistake in calculation on the part of the writer. Of course the writer is occasionally placed in an awkward position. A dramatic episode is about to take place, or, more correctly, the author wishes it to take place, but the characters have been dispersed about the map, and time and distance conspire against the author's purpose. It is madness to "blur" the positions and "risk" the reader's acuteness, but it is almost equally unfortunate to fail in observing the difficulty, and write on in blissful ignorance of the fact that nature's laws have been set at defiance. The drawing of a map, as before suggested, will obviate all these troubles.

Should you depict a lover's scene in India, take care not to describe it as occurring in "beautiful twilight." It is quite possible to know that darkness follows sunset, and yet to forget it in the moment of writing; but a good writer is never caught "napping" in these matters. If you don't know India, choose Cairo, about which, after half-a-dozen lengthened visits, you can speak with certainty.

SCIENTIFIC FACTS

What a nuisance the weather is to many novelists. Some triumph over their difficulties; a few contribute to our amusement. The meteorology of fiction would be a fascinating study. In second-rate productions, it is astonishing to witness the ease with which the weather is ordered about. The writer makes it rain when he thinks the incidents of a downpour will enliven the narrative, forgetting that the movement of the story, as previously stated, requires a blue sky and a shining sun; or he contrives to have the wind blowing in two or three directions at once. The sun and the moon require careful manipulation. At the beginning of a novel, the room of an invalid is said to have a window looking directly towards the east; but at the end of the book when the invalid dies, the author, wishing to make him depart this life in a flood of glory, suffuses this eastern-windowed room with "the red glare of the setting sun." The detail may appear unimportant, but it is not so, and a few hours devoted to notes on these minor points would save all the unpleasantness and ridicule which such mistakes too frequently bring. The reviewer loves to descant on the "peculiar cosmology and physical science of the volume before us."

The moon is most unfortunate. Mrs Humphry Ward confesses that she never knows when to make the moon rise, and obtains Miss Ward's assistance in all astronomical references. This is, of course, a pleasant exaggeration, but it shows that no venture should be made in science without being perfectly sure of your ground.

GRAMMAR

Grammar is the most dangerous of all pitfalls. Suppose you read your novel through, and check each sentence. After weary toil you are ready to offer a prize of one guinea to the man who can show you a mistake. When the full list of errors is drawn up by an expert grammarian, you are glad that offer was not made, for your guineas would have been going too quickly. In everyday conversation you speak as other people do—having a special hatred of painful accuracy, otherwise called pedantry; and as you frequently hear the phrase: "Those sort of people are never nice," it does not strike you as being incorrect when you read it in your proof-sheets. Or somebody refers to a theatrical performance, and regretting his inability to be present, says, "I should like to have gone, but could not." So often is the phrase used in daily speech, that its sound (when you read your book aloud) does not suggest anything erroneous. And yet if you wish your reader to know that you are a good grammarian, you will not be ashamed to revise your grammar and say, "I should have liked to go, but could not." These are simple instances: there are hundreds more.

Reviewing all that has been said in this chapter, the one conclusion is that the novelist must be a man of knowledge; he must know the English language from base to summit; and whatever references he makes to science, art, history, theology, or any other subject, he should have what is expected of writers in these specific departments—accuracy.

Chapter VIII

The Secret of Style

COMMUNICABLE ELEMENTS

One can readily sympathise with the melancholy of a man who, after reading De Quincey, Macaulay, Addison, Lamb, Pater, and Stevenson, found that literary style was still a mystery to him. He was obliged to confess that the secret of style is with them that have it. His main difficulty, however, was to reconcile this conviction with the advice of a learned friend who urged him to study the best models if he would attain a good style. Was style communicable? or was it not? Now of all questions relating to this subject, this is the most pertinent, and, if I may say so, the only real question. It is the easiest thing in the world to tell a student about Flaubert and Guy de Maupassant, about Tolstoi and Turgenieff, but no quantity of advice as to reading is of much avail unless the preliminary question just referred to is intelligently answered. The so-called stylists of all ages may be carefully read from beginning to end, and yet style will not disclose its secret. Such a course of reading could not but be beneficial; to live among the lovely things of literature would develop the taste and educate appreciation; the reader would be quick to discern beauty when he saw it, but the art of producing it other than by deliberate imitation of known models would be still a mystery.

Is style communicable? The answer is *Yes* and *No*; in some senses it is, in others it is not. Let us deal with the affirmative side first. This concerns all points of grammar and composition without which the story would not be clear and forcible. No writer can make a "corner" in the facts of grammar and composition; it is impossible to appropriate them individually to the exclusion of everybody else; and since style depends to some extent on a knowledge of those rules which govern the use of language, it follows that there are certain elements which are open to all who are willing to learn them. For instance, there is the study of words. How often do we hear it said of a certain novelist that he uses the right word with unerring accuracy. And this is regarded as an important feature in his style; therefore words and their uses should have a prominent place in your programme. In "The Silverado Squatters," Stevenson represents himself as carrying a pail of water up a hill: "the water *lipping* over the side, and a *quivering* sunbeam in the midst." The words in italics are the exact words wanted; no others could possibly set forth the facts with greater accuracy. Stevenson was a diligent word-student, and had a certain knowledge of their dynamic and suggestive qualities.

The right word! How shall we find it? Sometimes it will come with the thought; more often we must seek it. Landor says: "I hate false words, and seek with care, difficulty, and moroseness those that fit the thing." What could be stronger than the language of Guy de Maupassant? "Whatever the thing we wish to say there is but one word to express it, but one verb to give it movement, but one adjective to qualify it. We must seek till we find this noun, this verb, this adjective, and never allow ourselves to play tricks, even happy ones, or have recourse to sleights of language to avoid a difficulty. The subtlest things may be rendered and suggested by applying the hint conveyed in Boileau's line, 'He taught the power of a word in the right place.'" In similar vein, Professor Raleigh remarks, "Let the truth be said outright: there are no synonyms, and the same statement can never be repeated in a changed form of words."

The number of words used is another consideration. When Phil May has drawn a picture he proceeds to make erasures here and there with a view to retaining wholeness of effect by the least possible number of lines. There is a similar excellence in literature, the literature where "there is not a superfluous word." Oh, the "gasiness" of many a modern novel—pages and pages of so-called "style," "word-painting," and "description."

The conclusion of the matter is this: the right number of words, and each word in its place. Frederic Schlegel used to say that in good prose every word should be underlined; as if he had said that the interpretation of a sentence should not depend on the manner in which it is read.

It is also highly necessary that the would-be stylist should be a student of sentences and paragraphs. Surprising as it may seem, it is nevertheless true that many aspirants after literary success never give these matters a thought; they expect that proficiency will "come." Proficiency is not an angel who visits us unsolicited; it is a power that must be paid for with a price, and the price is laborious study of such practical technique as the following:—"In a series of sentences the stress should be varied continually so as to come in the beginning of some sentences, and at the end of others, regard being had for the two considerations, variation of rhythm, and grouping of similar ideas together." And this, "Every paragraph is subject to the general laws of unity, selection, proportion, sequence, and variety which govern all good composition." The observance of these rules (and they are specimens of hundreds more) and the discovery of apt illustrations in literature are matters of time and labour. But the time and labour are well spent— nay, they are absolutely necessary if the literary man would know his craft thoroughly. For the ordinary man, something equivalent to a text-book course in rhetoric is indispensable. True, many writers have learned insensibly from other writers, but too severe a devotion to the masterpieces of literature may beget the master's weaknesses without imparting his strength.

INCOMMUNICABLE ELEMENTS

The incommunicable element in style is that personal impress which a writer sets upon his work. What is a personal impress? I am asked. Can it be defined? Scarcely. Personality itself is a mysterious thing. We know what it means when it is used to distinguish a remarkable man from those who are not remarkable. "He has a unique personality," we say. Now that personality—if the man be a writer—will show itself in his literary offspring. It will be in evidence over and above rule, regulation, canons of art, and the like. If there be such a thing as a mystic presence, then style is that mystic presence of the writer's personality which permeates the ideas and language in such a way as to give them a distinction and individuality all their own. I will employ comparison as a means of illustration by supposing that the three following passages appeared in the same book in separate paragraphs and without the authors' names:—

"Each material thing has its celestial side, has its translation into the spiritual and necessary sphere, where it plays a part as indestructible as any other, and to these ends all things continually ascend. The gases gather to the solid firmament; the chemic lump arrives at the plant and grows; arrives at the quadruped and walks; arrives at the man and thinks."

"He [Daniel Webster] is a magnificent specimen; you might say to all the world, 'This is your Yankee Englishman; such limbs we make in Yankeeland! The tanned complexion; the amorphous crag-like face; the dull black eyes under their precipice of brows, like dull anthracite furnaces, needing only to be blown; the mastiff mouth, accurately closed:—I have not traced so much silent Bersekir rage that I remember of in any man.'"

"In the edifices of Man there should be found reverent worship and following, not only of the Spirit which rounds the form of the forest, and arches the vault of the avenue,—which gives veining to the leaf and polish to the shell, and grace to every pulse that agitates animal organisation—but of that also which reproves the pillars of the earth and builds up her barren precipices into the coldness of the clouds, and lifts her shadowy cones of mountain purple into the pale arch of the sky."

Now, an experienced writer, or reader, would identify these quotations at once; in some measure from a knowledge of the books from which they are taken, but mostly from a recognition of style pure and simple. The merest tyro can see that the passages are not the work of one author; there is, apart from subject-matter, a subtle something that lies hidden beneath the language, informing each paragraph with a style peculiar to itself. What is it? Ah! *The style is the man.* It is composition charged with personality. Emerson, Carlyle, and Ruskin used the English language with due regard for the rules of grammar, and such principles of literary art as they felt to be necessary. And yet when Emerson philosophises he does it in a way quite different to everybody else; when Carlyle analyses a character, you know without the Sage's signature that the work is his; and when Ruskin describes natural beauties by speaking of "shadowy cones of mountain purple" being lifted "into the pale arch of the sky"—well, that is Ruskin—it could be no other. In each case language is made the bearer of the writer's personality. Style in literature is the breathing forth of soul and spirit; as is the soul, and as is the spirit in depth, sympathy, and power, so will the style be rich, distinctive, and memorable. Professor Raleigh says that "All style is gesture—the gesture of the mind and of the soul. Mind we have in common, inasmuch as the laws of right reason are not different for different minds. Therefore clearness and arrangement can be taught, sheer incompetence in the art of expression can be partly remedied. But who shall impose laws on the soul? . . . Write, and after you have attained to some control over the instrument, you write yourself down whether you will or no. There is no vice, however unconscious, no virtue, however shy, no touch of meanness or of generosity in your character that will not pass on to paper." Hence the oft-repeated call for sincerity on the part of writers. If you try to imitate Hardy it is a literary hypocrisy, and your sin will find you out. If you are Meredith-minded, and play the sedulous ape to him, you must expect a similar catastrophe.

If the style is the man, how can you hope to equal that style if you can never come near the man?

Be true to all you know, and see, and feel; live with the masters, and catch their spirit. You will then get your own style—it may not be as good as those you have so long admired, but it will be *yours*; and, truth to tell, that is all you can hope for.

Chapter IX

How Authors Work

QUICK AND SLOW

The public has shown a deep interest in all details respecting the way in which writers produce their books; the food they eat, the clothes they wear, their weaknesses and their hobbies, what pens they use, and whether they prefer the typewriter or not—all these are items which a greedy public expects to know. So much is this the case to-day that an acrid critic recently offered the tart suggestion that a novelist was a man who wrote a great book, and spent the rest of his time—very profitably—in telling the world how he came to write it. I do not intend to pander to the literary news-monger in these pages, but to reproduce as much as I know of the way in which novelists work, in order to throw out hints as to how a beginner may perchance better his own methods. A word of warning, however, is necessary. Do not, for Heaven's sake, *ape* anybody. Because Zola darkens his rooms when he writes, that is no reason why you should go and do likewise; and if John Fiske likes to sit in a draught, pray save yourself the expense of a doctor's bill by imitating him. An author's methods are only of service to a novice when they enable him to improve his own; and it is with this object in view that I reproduce the following personal notes.

The relative speeds of the writing fraternity are little short of amazing. Hawthorne was slow in composing. Sometimes he wrote only what amounted to half-a-dozen pages a week, often only a few lines in the same space of time, and, alas! he frequently went to his chamber and took up his pen only to find himself wholly unable to perform any literary work. Bret Harte has been known to pass days and weeks on a short story or poem before he was ready to deliver it into the hands of the printer. Thomas Hardy is said to have spent seven years in writing "Jude the Obscure." On the other hand, Victor Hugo wrote his "Cromwell" in three months, and his "Notre Dame de Paris" in four months and a half. Wilkie Collins, prince among the plotters, was accustomed to compose at white heat. Speaking of "Heart and Science," he says: "Rest was impossible. I made a desperate effort, rushed to the sea, went sailing and fishing, and was writing my book all the time 'in my head,' as the children say. The one wise course to take was to go back to my desk and empty my head, and then rest. My nerves are too much shaken for travelling. An arm-chair and a cigar, and a hundred and fiftieth reading of the glorious Walter Scott—King, Emperor, and President of Novelists—there is the regimen that is doing me good." An enterprising editor, not very long ago, sent out circulars to prominent authors asking them how much they can do in a day. The reply in most cases was that the rate of production varied; sometimes the pen or the typewriter could not keep pace with thought; at other times it was just the opposite.

It is very necessary at this point to draw a distinction between the execution of a work, and its development in the mind from birth to full perfection. When we read that Mr Crockett, or somebody else, produced so many books in so many years, it does not always mean—if ever—that the idea and its expression have been a matter of weeks or months. To *write* a novel in six weeks is not an impossibility—even a passable novel; but to sit down and think out a plot, with all its details of character and event, and to write it out so that in six weeks, or two or three months, the MS. is on the publisher's desk—well, don't believe it. No novel worthy of the name was ever produced at that rate.

HOW MANY WORDS A DAY?

In nothing do authors differ so much as on the eternal problem of whether it is right to produce a certain quantity of matter every day—inspiration or no inspiration. Thomas Hardy has no definite hours for working, and, although he often uses the night-time for this purpose, he has a preference for the day-time. Charlotte Brontë had to choose favourable seasons for literary work—"weeks, sometimes months, elapsed before she felt that she had anything to add to that portion of her story which was already written; then some morning she would wake up and the progress of her tale lay clear and bright before her in distinct vision, and she set to work to write out what was more present to her mind at such times than actual life was."[17] When writing "Jane Eyre," and little Jane had been brought to Thornfield, the author's enthusiasm had grown so great that she could not stop. She went on incessantly for weeks.

Miss Jane Barlow confesses that she is "a very slow worker; indeed, when I consider the amount of work which the majority of writers turn out in a year, I feel that I must be dreadfully lazy. Even in my quiet life here I find it difficult to get a long, clear space of time for my work, and the slightest interruption will upset me for hours. It is difficult to make people understand that it is not so much the time they take up, as causing me to break the line of thought. It may be that somebody only comes into the study to speak to me for a minute, but it is quite enough. I suppose it is very silly to be so sensitive to interruptions, but I cannot help it. I sometimes say it is as though a box of beads had been upset, and I had to gather them together again; that is just the effect of anyone speaking to me when I am at work. I write everything by hand, and it takes a long time. I am sure I could not use a typewriter, or dictate; indeed, I never let anybody see what I have written until it is in print. Sometimes I write a passage over a dozen times before it comes right, and I always make a second copy of everything, but the corrections are not very numerous."

Mr William Black was also a slow producer: "I am building up a book months before I write the first chapter;

---

17. Erichsen: "Methods of Authors."

before I can put pen to paper I have to realise all the chief incidents and characters. I have to live with my characters, so to speak; otherwise, I am afraid they would never appear living people to my readers. This is my work during the summer; the only time I am free from the novel that-is-to-be is when I am grouse-shooting or salmon-fishing. At other times I am haunted by the characters and the scenes in which they take part, so that, for the sake of his peace of mind, my method is not to be recommended to the young novelist. When I come to the writing, I have to immure myself in perfect quietude; my study is at the top of the house, and on the two or three days a week I am writing, Mrs Black guards me from interruption. . . . Of course, now and again, I have had to read a good deal preparatory to writing. Before beginning 'Sunrise,' for instance, I went through the history of secret societies in Europe."

CHARLES READE AND ANTHONY TROLLOPE

"Charles Reade's habit of working was unique. When he had decided on a new work, he plotted out the scheme, situations, facts, and characters on three large sheets of pasteboard. Then he set to work, using very large foolscap to write on, working rapidly, but with frequent references to his storehouse of facts in the scrap-books which were ready at his hand. The genial novelist was a great reader of newspapers. Anything that struck him as interesting, or any fact which tended to support one of his humanitarian theories, was cut out, pasted in a large folio scrap-book, and carefully indexed. Facts of any sort were his hobby.

From the scrap-books thus collected with great care, he used to 'elaborate' the questions treated of in his novels."

Anthony Trollope is one of the few men who have taken their readers into their full confidence about book production. The quotation I am about to make is rather long, but it is too detailed to be shortened:

"When I have commenced a new book I have always prepared a diary, divided into weeks, and carried it on for the period which I have allowed myself for the completion of the work. In this I have entered day by day the number of pages I have written, so that if at any time I have slipped into idleness for a day or two, the record of that idleness has been there staring me in the face, and demanding of me increased labour, so that the deficiency might be supplied. According to the circumstances of the time, whether any other business might be then heavy or light, or whether the book which I was writing was, or was not, wanted with speed, I have allotted myself so many pages a week. The average number has been about forty. It has been placed as low as twenty, and has risen to one hundred and twelve. And as a page is an ambiguous term, my page has been made to contain two hundred and fifty words, and as words, if not watched, will have a tendency to straggle, I have had every word counted as I went."[18]

Under the title of "A Walk in the Wood," Trollope thus describes his method of plot-making, and the difficulty the novelist experiences in making the "tricksy Ariel"

---

18 "Autobiography," vol. ii.

of the imagination do his bidding. "I have to confess that my incidents are fabricated to fit my story as it goes on, and not my story to fit my incidents. I wrote a novel once in which a lady forged a will, but I had not myself decided that she had forged it till the chapter before that in which she confesses her guilt. In another, a lady is made to steal her own diamonds, a grand *tour de force*, as I thought, but the brilliant idea struck me only when I was writing the page in which the theft is described. I once heard an unknown critic abuse my workmanship because a certain lady had been made to appear too frequently in my pages. I went home and killed her immediately. I say this to show that the process of thinking to which I am alluding has not generally been applied to any great effort of construction. It has expended itself on the minute ramifications of tale-telling: how this young lady should be made to behave herself with that young gentleman; how this mother or that father would be affected by the ill conduct or the good of a son or a daughter; how these words or those other would be most appropriate or true to nature if used on some special occasion. Such plottings as these with a fabricator of fiction are infinite in number, but not one of them can be done fitly without thinking. My little effort will miss its wished-for result unless I be true to nature; and to be true to nature, I must think what nature would produce. Where shall I go to find my thoughts with the greatest ease and most perfect freedom?

"I have found that I can best command my thoughts on foot, and can do so with the most perfect mastery when wandering through a wood. To be alone is, of course, essential. Companionship requires conversation, for which, indeed, the spot is most fit; but conversation is not now the object in view. I have found it best even to reject the society of a dog, who, if he be a dog of manners, will make some attempt at talking; and, though he should be silent, the sight of him provokes words and caresses and sport. It is best to be away from cottages, away from children, away as far as may be from chance wanderers. So much easier is it to speak than to think, that any slightest temptation suffices to carry away the idler from the harder to the lighter work. An old woman with a bundle of sticks becomes an agreeable companion, or a little girl picking wild fruit. Even when quite alone, when all the surroundings seem to be fitted for thought, the thinker will still find a difficulty in thinking. It is easy to lose an hour in maundering over the past, and to waste the good things which have been provided, in remembering instead of creating!"

THE MISSION OF FANCY

"It is not for rules of construction that the writer is seeking, as he roams listlessly or walks rapidly through the trees. These have come to him from much observation, from the writings of others, from that which we call study, in which imagination has but little immediate concern. It is the fitting of the rules to the characters which he has created, the filling in with living touches and true colours those daubs and blotches on his canvas which have been easily scribbled with a rough hand, that the true work consists. It is here that he requires that his fancy should be undisturbed, that the trees should overshadow him, that the birds should comfort him, that the green and yellow mosses should be in unison with him, that the very air should be good to him. The rules are there fixed—fixed as far as his judgment can fix them—and are no longer a difficulty to him. The first coarse outlines of his story he has found to be a matter almost indifferent to him. It is with these little plottings that he has to contend. It is for them that he must catch his Ariel and bind him fast, and yet so bind him that not a thread shall touch the easy action of his wings. Every little scene must be arranged so that—if it may be possible—the proper words may be spoken, and the fitting effect produced."

FANCIES OF ANOTHER TYPE

Most authors indulge in little eccentricities when working, and, if the time should ever come that your name is brought before the public notice, it would be advisable to develop some whimsical habit so as to be prepared for the interviewer, who is sure to ask whether you have one. To push your pen through your hair during creative moments would be a good plan; it would reveal a line of baldness where you had furrowed the hair off, and afford ocular proof to all and sundry that you possessed a genuine eccentricity. Or if you prefer a habit still more *bizarre*, you might put a hammock in a tree, and always write your most exciting scenes during a rain-storm, and under the shelter of a dripping umbrella.

The fact is, every penman has his little peculiarities when at work, but they should be kept as private property. Of course, there are authors who revel in publicity, and others again have intimate details wormed out of them. The fact remains, however, that these details are interesting, because they are personal; and they are occasionally helpful, because they enable one writer to compare notes with others. We have all heard of the methodical habits of Kant. When thinking out his deep thoughts, he always placed himself so that his eyes might fall on a certain old tower. This old tower became so necessary to his thoughts, that when some poplar trees grew up and hid it from his sight, he found himself unable to think at all, until, at his earnest request, the trees were cropped and the tower was brought into sight again.

George Eliot was very susceptible as to her surroundings. When about to write, she dressed herself with great care, and arranged her harmoniously-furnished room in perfect order.[19] Hawthorne had a habit of cutting some article while composing. He is said to have taken a garment from his wife's sewing-basket, and cut it into pieces without being conscious of the act. Thus an entire table and the arms of a rocking-chair were whittled away in this manner.

Upon Ibsen's writing-table is a small tray containing a number of grotesque figures—a wooden bear, a tiny devil, two or three cats (one of them playing a fiddle), and some rabbits. Ibsen has said: "I never write a single line of any of my dramas without having that tray and its occupants before me on my table. I could not write without them. But why I use them is my own secret."

---

19. Erichsen: "Methods of Authors."

Ouida writes in the early morning. She gets up at five o'clock, and before she begins, works herself up into a sort of literary trance. Maurice Jokai always uses violet ink, to which he is so accustomed that he becomes perplexed when compelled, outside of his own house, to resort to ink of another colour. He claims that thoughts are not forthcoming when he writes with any other ink. One of the corners of his writing-desk holds a miniature library, consisting of neatly-bound note-books which contain the outline of his novels as they originated in his mind. When he has once begun a romance, he keeps right on until it is completed.

SOME OF OUR YOUNGER WRITERS

Mr Zangwill has no particular method of working; he works in spasms. Regular hours, he says, may be possible to a writer of pure romance, but if you are writing of the life about you, such regularity is impossible.[20] Coulson Kernahan works in the morning and in the evening, but never in the afternoon. He always reserves the afternoon for walking, cycling, and exercise generally. He is unable to work regularly; some days indeed pass without doing a stroke.[21] Anthony Hope is found at his desk every morning, but if the inspiration does not come, he never forces himself to write. Sometimes it will come after waiting several hours, and sometimes it will seem to have come when it hasn't, which means that next morning he has to tear up

---

20. Interview in *The Young Man*, by Percy L. Parker.
21. Interview in *The Young Man*, by A. H. Lawrence.

what was written the day before and start afresh.[22] Before
Robert Barr publishes a novel he spends years in thinking
the thing out. In this way ten years were spent over "The
Mutable Many," and two more years in writing it.[23] When
Max Pemberton has a book in the making he just sits down
and writes away at it when in the mood. "I find," he says,
"that I can always work best in the morning. One's brain is
fresher and one's ideas come more readily. If I work at night
I find that I have to undo a great deal of it in the morning.
In working late at night I have done so under the impression that I have accomplished some really fine work, only
to rise in the morning and, after looking at it, feel that one
ought to shed tears over such stuff."[24] H. G. Wells, as might
be expected, has a way of his own. "In the morning I merely revise proofs and type-written copy, and write letters,
and, in fact, any work that does not require the exercise
of much imagination. If it is fine, I either have a walk or a
ride on the cycle. We also have a tandem, and sometimes
my wife and I take the double machine out; and then after
lunch we have tea about half-past three in the afternoon. It
is after this cup of tea that I do my work. The afternoon is
the best time of the day for me, and I nearly always work
on until eight o'clock, when we have dinner. If I am working at something in which I feel keenly interested, I work
on from nine o'clock until after midnight, but it is on the
afternoon work that my output mainly depends."[25]

----

22. Interview in *The Young Man*, by Sarah A. Tooley.
23. *Ibid.*
24. Interview in *The Young Man*, by A. H. Lawrence.
25. Interview in *The Young Man*, by A. H. Lawrence.

CURIOUS METHODS

In another interview Mr Wells said, "I write and re-write. If you want to get an effect, it seems to me that the first thing you have to do is to write the thing down as it comes into your mind" ("slush," Mr Wells calls it), "and so get some idea of the shape of it. In this preliminary process, no doubt, one can write a good many thousand words a day, perhaps seven or eight thousand. But when all that is finished, it will take you seven or eight solid days to pick it to pieces again, and knock it straight.

"The 'slush' effort of 'The Invisible Man' came to more than 100,000 words; the final outcome of it amounts to 55,000. My first tendency was to make it much shorter still.

"I used to feel a great deal ashamed of this method. I thought it simply showed incapacity, and inability to hit the right nail on the head. The process is like this:

"(1) Worry and confusion.

"(2) Testing the idea, and trying to settle the question. Is the idea any good?

"(3) Throwing the idea away; getting another; finally returning, perhaps, to the first.

"(4) The next thing is possibly a bad start.

"(5) Grappling with the idea with the feeling that it has to be done.

"(6) Then the slush work, which I've already described.

"(7) Reading this over, and taking out what you think is essential, and re-writing the essential part of it.

"(8) After it has been type-written, you cut it about, so that it has to be re-typed.

"(9) The result of your labour finds its way into print, and you take hold of the first opportunity to go over the whole thing again."[26]

Contrasted with the pleasant humour of the above is the gravity of Ian Maclaren. "Although the stories I have written may seem very simple, they are very laboriously done. This kind of short story cannot be done quickly. There is no plot, no incident, and one has to depend entirely upon character and slight touches, curiously arranged and bound together, to produce the effect. . . . Each of the 'Bonnie Brier Bush' stories went through these processes:—

(1) Slowly drafted arrangement;

(2) draft revised before writing;

(3) written;

(4) manuscript revised;

(5) first proof corrected;

(6) revise corrected;

---

26. Interview in *To-Day,* for September 11th, 1897, by A. H. Lawrence.

(7) having been published in a periodical, revised for book;

(8) first proof corrected;

(9) second proof corrected."[27]

Enough. These personal notes will teach the novice that every man must make and follow his own plan of work. Experience is the best guide and the wisest teacher.

27. Interview in *The Christian Commonwealth* for September 24th, 1896.

Chapter X

Is the Subject-Matter of Novels Exhausted?

THE QUESTION STATED

This is the way in which the question is most often stated, but the real question is more intelligently expressed by asking: Has the novel, as a form of literature, become obsolete? or is it likely to be obsolete in the near future? To many people the matter is dismissed with a contemptuous *Pshaw!*; others think it worthy of serious inquiry, and a few with practical minds say they don't care whether it is or not. Seven years ago Mr Frederic Harrison delivered himself of very pessimistic views as to the present position and prospects of the novelist, and not long ago Mr A. J. Balfour asserted that in his opinion the art of fiction had reached its zenith, and was now in its decline. These critics may be prejudiced in their views, but it is worth while considering the remarks of the one who has the greater claim to respect for literary judgment. After exclaiming that we have now no novelist of the first rank, and substantiating this statement to the best of his ability, Mr Harrison goes on to inquire into the causes of this decay. In the first place, we have too high a standard of taste and criticism. "A highly organised code of culture may give us good manners, but it is the death of genius." We have lost the true sense of the romantic, and if "Jane Eyre" were produced to-day it "would not rise above a common shocker." Secondly, we are too disturbed in political affairs to allow for the rest that is necessary for literary productiveness. Thirdly, life is not so dramatic as it was—character is being driven inwards, and we have lost the picturesque qualities of earlier days.

I am not at present concerned with the truth or error of these arguments; my object just now is to state the case, and before proceeding to an examination of its merits I wish to take the testimony of another writer and thinker, one who is a philosopher quite as much as the author of "The Foundations of Belief" or the author of "The Meaning of History," and who has a claim upon our attention as an investigator of moving causes.

Mr C. H. Pearson, in his notable book, "National Life and Character," has made some confident statements on the subject of the exhaustion of literary products. He is of opinion that "a change in social relations has made the drama impossible by dwarfing the immediate agency of the individual," and that "a change in manners has robbed the drama of a great deal of effect." He goes on to say that "Human nature, various as it is, is only capable after all of a certain number of emotions and acts, and these as the topics of an incessant literature are bound after a time to be exhausted. We may say with absolute certainty that certain subjects are never to be taken again. The tale of Troy, the wanderings of Odysseus, the vision of Heaven and Hell as Dante saw it, the theme of 'Paradise Lost,' and the story of Faust are familiar instances. . . . Effective adaptations of an old subject may still be possible; but it is not writers of the highest capacity who will attempt them, and the reading world, which remembers what has been done before, will never accord more than a secondary recognition to the adaptation".

There is a curious atmosphere of logical conclusiveness about these arguments. They carry with them, apparently, an air of certainty which it is useless to question. We know that the novelist has already exploited Politics, Socialism, History, Theology, Marriage, Education, and a host of other subjects; indeed, a perusal of Dixon's "Index to Fiction" is calculated to provoke the inquiry: "Is there anything left to write about?" We know that everywhere is springing up the "literature of locality," and it would seem as if the resources of this world's experience had been exhausted when writers like Mr H. G. Wells and the late George Du Maurier invade the planet Mars for fresh material. The heavens above, the earth beneath, and the waters under the earth have all been "written up." Is there anything new?

"CHANGE" NOT "EXHAUSTION"

There can be no doubt that fiction has undergone great changes during recent years. These changes are the result of deeper changes in our common life. Consider for a moment the position of the drama. What is the significance of the problem play on the one hand, and the cry for a "Static Theatre" on the other hand? It means that life has changed, and is still changing; that the national character is not so emphatically external or spontaneous as in those days when Ben Jonson killed two men, and Marlowe himself was killed in a brawl. We have lost the passion, the force, and the brutality of those times, and have become more contemplative and analytical. The simple law is this: that literature and the drama are a reflex of life; hence, when character has a tendency to be driven inwards, as is the case to-day, Maeterlinck pleads on behalf of a drama without action; and Paul Bourget in France and Henry James in England embody the spirit of the age in the fiction of psychological minutiæ. Now there may be symptoms of decay in these manifestations of literary impulse, but the impulse is part of that new experience which the facts of an increasingly complex civilisation foist upon us. And, further, *change* is not necessarily *exhaustion*; in fact, it is more than surprising that anyone can believe all the stories possible have been told already, or have been told in the most interesting way. It is a very ancient cry—this cry about exhaustion. The old Hebrew writer wailed something about wanting to meet with a man who could show him a new thing. A new thing? "There is no new thing under the Sun." But we have found a few since those days, and the future will give birth to as many more.

Men and women have written about love from time immemorial, but have we finished with the theme? Is it exhausted? Did Homer satisfy our love of recorded adventure once and for all? There is only one answer—namely, that human experience is infinite in its possibilities and its capacity for renewal. If human experience—these vague and subtle emotions, these violently real but inscrutable feelings, these tremulous questionings of existence encompassed with mystery—if human experience were no more than a hard and dry scientific fact, well, our novelists would have a poor time of it. But life knows no finality; its stream flows on in perennial flood. Human nature is said to be much the same the world over, and yet every personality is absolutely a new thing. Goethe might attempt a rough classification by saying we are either Platonists or Aristotelians, but actually a great many of us are neither one nor the other, and there are infinities of degrees amongst us even then. New character is a necessary outcome of the advancing centuries, and new personalities are being born every day.

No; the world still loves a story, and there are stories which have never been told. It is, perhaps, true, that the story-tellers have not found them yet. Why?

WHY WE TALK ABOUT EXHAUSTION

The answer is: We are becoming too artificial; we are losing spontaneity, and are getting too far away from the soil. Have we not noticed over and over again that the first book of a novelist is his best? Those which followed are called "good," but they sell because the author is the author of the first book which created a sensation.

Speaking of the first work of a young writer, Anthony Trollope says: "He sits down and tells his story because he has a story to tell; as you, my friend, when you have heard something which has at once tickled your fancy or moved your pathos, will hurry to tell it to the first person you meet. But when that first novel has been received graciously by the public, and has made for itself a success, then the writer, naturally feeling that the writing of novels is within his grasp, looks about for something to tell in another. He cudgels his brains, not always successfully, and sits down to write, not because he has something which he burns to tell, but because he feels it to be incumbent on him to be telling something. . . . So it has been with many novelists, who, after some good work, perhaps after much good work, have distressed their audience because they have gone on with their work till their work has become simply a trade with them."[28] There is often a good reason for such a change. The first book was written in a place near to Nature's heart; the writer was free from the obligations of society as found in city life; he was thrown back on his own resources, and fortunately could not spoil his individual view of things by multitudinous references to books and authorities. Do we not selfishly wish that Miss Olive Schreiner had never left the veldt, in the loneliness of which she produced "The Story of an African Farm"? Nearer contact with civilisation has failed to induce an impulse the result of which is at all comparable with this genuine story. It may or may not be of significance that Mr Wells, the creator of a distinct type of

---

28. "Autobiography," vol. ii. pp. 45-6. There is no harm in telling stories as a trade provided the stories are good.

romance, dislikes what is called "Society," but I fancy that a few of those who lament too frequently that "everything has been said" spend more time in "Society" and clubs than is possible for good work. Mr C. H. Pearson, in a notable chapter on "Dangers of Political Development," says: "The world at large is just as reverent of greatness, as observant of a Browning, a Newman, or a Mill, as it ever was; but the world of Society prefers the small change of available and ephemeral talent to the wealth of great thoughts, which must always be kept more or less in reserve. The result seems to be that men, anxious to do great work, find city life less congenial than they did, and either live away from the Metropolis, as Darwin and Newman did, or restrict their intercourse, as Carlyle and George Eliot practically did, to a circle of chosen friends."

In further confirmation of the position I have taken up, let me quote the testimony of Thomas Hardy as given in an interview. Said the interviewer—"In reading 'A Group of Noble Dames,' I was struck with the waste of good material."

"Yes," replied Mr Hardy, "I suppose I was wasteful. But, there! it doesn't matter, for I have far more material now than I shall ever be able to use."

"In your note-books?"

"Yes, and in my head. I don't believe in that idea of man's imaginative powers becoming naturally exhausted; I believe that, if he liked, a man could go on writing till his physical strength gave out. Most men exhaust themselves prematurely by something artificial—their manner of living—Scott and Dickens for example. Victor Hugo, on the other hand, who was so long in exile, and who necessarily lived a very simple life during much of his time, was writing as well as ever when he died at a good old age. So, too, was Carlyle, if we except his philosophy, the least interesting part of him. The great secret is perhaps for the writer to be content with the life he was living when he made his first success. I can do more work here [in Dorsetshire] in six months than in twelve months in London."[29]

These are the convictions of a strong man, one who stands at the head of English writers of fiction, and therefore one to whom the beginner especially should listen with respect. A reader of MSS. told me quite recently that there was a pitiable narrowness of experience in the productions which were handed to him for valuation; nearly all were cast in the "city" mould, and showed signs of having been written to say something rather than because the writers had something to say. Mr Hardy has put his finger on the weak spot: more stories "come" in the country stillness than in the city's bustle. Of course, a man can be as much of a hermit in the heart of London as in the heart of a forest, but how few can resist the attractions of Society and the temptation to multiply literary friendships! Besides, it is always a risk to make a permanent change in that environment which assisted in producing the first success. Follow Mr Hardy's advice and stay where you are. Stories will then not be slow to "come" and ideas to "occur"; and the pessi-

29. Interview in *The Young Man.*

mists will be less ready to utter their laments over the decadence of fiction and philosophers to argue that the novel will soon become extinct. I cannot do better than close with the following tempered statement from Mr Edmund Gosse: "A question which constantly recurs to my mind is this: Having secured the practical monopoly of literature, what do the novelists propose to do next? To what use will they put the unprecedented opportunity thrown in their way? It is quite plain that to a certain extent the material out of which the English novel has been constructed is in danger of becoming exhausted. Why do the American novelists inveigh against plots? Not, we may be sure, through any inherent tenderness of conscience, as they would have us believe; but because their eminently sane and somewhat timid natures revolt against the effort of inventing what is extravagant. But all the obvious plots, all the stories that are not in some degree extravagant, seem to have been told already, and for a writer of the temperament of Mr Howells, there is nothing left but the portraiture of a small portion of the limitless field of ordinary humdrum existence. So long as this is fresh, this also may amuse and please; to the practitioners of this kind of work it seems as though the infinite prairie of life might be surveyed thus for centuries acre by acre. But that is not possible. A very little while suffices to show that in this direction also the material is promptly exhausted. Novelty, freshness, and excitement are to be sought for at all hazards, and where can they be found? The novelists hope many things from that happy system of nature which supplies them year by year with fresh generations of the ingenuous young." In this, however, Mr Gosse is very doubtful of good results: the fact is, he is too pessimistic. But in making suggestions as to what kind of novels might be written he almost gives the lie to his previous opinions. He asks for novels addressed especially to middle-aged persons, and not to the ingenuous young, ever interested in love. "It is supposed that to describe one of the positive employments of life—a business or a profession for example—would alienate the tender reader, and check that circulation about which novelists talk as if they were delicate invalids. But what evidence is there to show that an attention to real things does frighten away the novel reader. The experiments which have been made in this country to widen the field of fiction in one direction, that of religious and moral speculation, have not proved unfortunate. What was the source of the great popular success of 'John Inglesant,' and then of 'Robert Elsmere,' if not the intense delight of readers in being admitted, in a story, to a wider analysis of the interior workings of the mind than is compatible with the mere record of billing and cooing of the callow young? . . . All I ask for is a larger study of life. Have the stress and turmoil of a political career no charm? Why, if novels of the shop and counting-house be considered sordid, can our novels not describe the life of a sailor, of a game-keeper, of a railway porter, of a civil engineer? What capital central figures for a story would be the whip of a leading hunt, the foreman of a colliery, the master of a fishing-smack, or a speculator on the Stock Exchange?"[30]

Since these words were written, the novel of politics, for example, has come to the fore; but does that mean

---

30. **"Questions at Issue,"** *The Tyranny of the Novel.*

that the subject is exhausted? It has only been touched upon as yet. There were plenty of dramas before Shakespeare but there were no Shakespeares; and to-day there are thousands of novels but how many real novelists? Once again let it be said that "exhausted subject-matter" is a misnomer; what we wait for is creative genius.

Chapter XI

THE NOVEL *v.* THE SHORT STORY

PRACTISE THE SHORT STORY

The beginner in fiction often asks: Is it not best to prepare for novel-writing by writing short stories? The question is much to the point, and merits a careful answer.

First of all, what is the difference between a novel and a short story? The difference lies in the point of view. The short story generally deals with one event in one particular life; the novel deals with many events in several lives, where both characters and action are dominated by one progressive purpose. To put it another way: the short story is like a miniature in painting, whilst the novel demands a much larger canvas. A suggestive paragraph from a review sets forth clearly the difference referred to: "The smaller your object of artistry, the nicer should be your touch, the more careful your attention to minutiæ. That, surely, would seem an axiom. You don't paint a miniature in the broad strokes that answer for a drop curtain, nor does the weaver of a pocket-handkerchief give to that fabric the texture of a carpet. But the usual writer of fiction, when it occurs to him to utilise one of his second best ideas in the manufacture of a short story, will commonly bring to his undertaking exactly the same slap-dash methods which he has found to serve in the construction of his novels. . . . Where he should have brought a finer method, he has brought a coarser; where he should have worked goldsmithwise, with tiny chisel, finishing exquisitely, he has worked blacksmithwise, with sledge hammer and anvil; where, because the thing is little, every detail counts, he has been slovenly in detail."[31]

It has been said that the novel deals with life from the inside, and short stories with life from the outside; but this is not so. Guy de Maupassant's "The Necklace" opens out to us a state of soul just as much as "Tess" does, even though it may be but a glimpse as compared with the prolonged exhibition of Mr Hardy's "pure woman."

Returning to the question previously referred to, one may well hesitate to advise a novice to commence writing short stories which demand such infinite care in conception and execution. The tendency of young writers is to verbosity—longwindedness in dialogues, in descriptions, and in delineations of character,—whereas the chief excellence of the story is the extent and depth of its suggestions as compared with its brevity in words. Should not a man perfect himself in the less minute and less delicate methods of the novel before he attempts the finer art of the short story?

There is a sound of good logic about all this, but it is not conclusive. Some men have a natural predilection

---

31. *Daily Chronicle*, June 22, 1899.

for the larger canvas and some for the smaller, so that the final decision cannot be forced upon anyone on purely abstract grounds; we must first know a writer's native capacity before advising him what to do. If you feel that literary art on a minute scale is your *forte*, then follow it enthusiastically, and work hard; if otherwise, act accordingly.

But, after all, there are certain abstract considerations which lead me to say that the short story should be practised before the novel. Take the very material fact of *size*. Have those who object to this recommendation ever thought of what practising novel-writing means? How long does it take to make a couple of experiments of 80,000 words each? A good deal, no doubt, depends on the man himself, but a quick writer would not do much to satisfy others at the rate of 160,000 words in twelve months. No, time is too precious for practising works of such length as these, and since the general principles of fiction apply to both novel and short story alike, the student cannot do better than practise his art in the briefer form. Moreover, if he is wise, he will seek the advice of experts, and (a further base consideration) it will be cheaper to have 4000 words criticised than a MS. containing 80,000.

Further, the foundation principles of the art of fiction cannot be learned more effectively, even for the purpose of writing novels, than in practising short stories. All the points brought forward in the preceding pages relating to plot, dialogue, proportion, climax, and so forth, are elements of the latter as well as of the former. If, as has been said, "windiness" is the chief fault of the beginner, where can he learn to correct that error more quickly? The art of knowing what to leave out is important to a novelist; it is more important to the short story writer; hence, if it be studied on the smaller canvas, it will be of excellent service when attempting the larger. "The attention to detail, the obliteration of the unessential, the concentration in expression, which the form of the short story demands, tends to a beneficent influence on the style of fiction. No one doubts that many of the great novelists of the past are somewhat tedious and prolix. The style of Richardson, Scott, Dumas, Balzac, and Dickens, when they are not at their strongest and highest, is often slipshod and slovenly; and such carelessly-worded passages as are everywhere in their works will scarcely be found in the novels of the future. The writers of short stories have made clear that the highest literary art knows neither synonyms, episodes, nor parentheses."[32]

SHORT STORY WRITERS ON THEIR ART

I cannot pretend to give more than a few hints as to the best way of following out the advice laid down in the foregoing paragraphs, and prefer to let some writers speak for themselves. Of course, it does not follow that Mr Wedmore can instruct a novice in literary art, simply because he can write exquisite short stories himself; indeed, it often happens that such men do not really know how they produce their work; but Mr Wedmore's article on *The Short Story* in his volume called "Books and Arts" is most profitable reading.

32.　*The International Monthly*, **vol. i.**

Some time ago a symposium appeared in a popular journal,[33] on the subject *How to Write a Short Story*. Mr Robert Barr could be no other than pithy in his recipe. He says: "It seems to me that a short story writer should act, metaphorically, like this—he should put his idea for a story into one cup of a pair of balances, then into the other he should deal out words—five hundred, a thousand, two thousand, three thousand, as the case may be—and when the number of words thus paid in causes the beam to rise on which his idea hangs, then his story is finished. If he puts a word more or less he is doing false work. . . . My model is Euclid, whose justly celebrated book of short stories entitled 'The Elements of Geometry' will live when most of us who are scribbling to-day are forgotten. Euclid lays down his plot, sets instantly to work at its development, letting no incident creep in that does not bear relation to the climax, using no unnecessary word, always keeping his one end in view, and the moment he reaches the culmination he stops." Mr Walter Raymond is apologetic. He fences a good deal, and pleads that the mention of "short story" is dangerous to his mental sequence, so much and so painfully has he tried to solve the problem of how one is written. Finally, however, he delivers himself of these pregnant sentences: "Show us the psychological moment; give us a sniff of the earth below; a glimpse of the sky above; and you will have produced a fine story. It need not exceed two thousand words."

The author of "Tales of Mean Streets" says: "The command of form is the first thing to be cultivated. Let

---

33. *The Young Man.*

the pupil take a story by a writer distinguished by the perfection of his workmanship—none could be better than Guy de Maupassant—and let him consider that story apart from the book as something happening before his eyes. Let him review mentally *everything* that happens— the things that are not written in the story as well as those that are—and let him review them, not necessarily in the order in which the story presents them, but in that in which they would come before an observer in real life. In short, from the fiction let him construct ordinary, natural, detailed, unselected, unarranged fact, making notes, if necessary, as he goes. Then let him compare his raw fact with the words of the master. He will see where the unessential is rejected; he will see how everything is given its just proportion in the design; he will perceive that every incident, every sentence, and every word has its value, its meaning, and its part in the whole."

Mr Morrison's ideas are endorsed by Miss Jane Barlow, Mr G. B. Burgin, Mr G. M. Fenn, and Mrs L. T. Meade. Mr Joseph Hocking does not seem to care for the brevity of short story methods. He cites eight lines which he heard some children sing:

"Little boy,
Pair of skates,
Broken ice,
Heaven's gates.
Little girl

Stole a plum,

Cholera bad,

Kingdom come,"

and remarks: "Many of our short stories are constructed on the principle of these verses. So few words are used, that the reader does not feel he is reading a story, but an outline." Mr Hocking has the British Public on his side, no doubt, but the great British Public is not always right, as he appears to believe.

I think if the reader will study the short stories of Guy de Maupassant and Mr Frederic Wedmore, and digest the advice given above, he will know enough to begin his work. Each experiment will enlarge his vision and discipline his pen, so that when he has accomplished something like tolerable success, he may safely attempt the larger canvas on the lines laid down in the preceding chapters.

Chapter XII

Success: And Some of its Minor Conditions

THE TRUTH ABOUT SUCCESS

There are two kinds of success in fiction—commercial and literary; and sometimes a writer is able to combine the two. Thomas Hardy is an example of the writer who produces literature and has large sales. On the other hand, there are many writers who succeed in one direction, but not in the other. The works of Marie Corelli have an amazing circulation, but they are not regarded as literature; whereas such genuine work as that of Mr Quiller Couch has to be content with sales far less extensive.

Now Thomas Hardy, Marie Corelli, and Quiller Couch have all succeeded, but in different ways. No doubt the reader would prefer to succeed in the manner of Hardy, but if he can't do it, he must be content to succeed in the best way he can. It is easy to talk about Miss Corelli's "rot" and "bosh" and "high falutin," but long columns of figures in a publisher's ledger mean something after all. They do not necessarily mean literary merit, delicate insight, or beautiful characterisation; they probably mean a keen sense of what the public likes, and a power to tickle its palate in an agreeable manner. Still, not every man or woman is able to do this, and although such a success may not rank as one of the first order, it *is* a success which nobody can gainsay. Literary journals have been instituting "inquiries" into the cases of men like Mr Silas Hocking and the Rev. E. P. Roe: why have they a circulation numbered by the million? No "inquiry" is needed. They are literary merchantmen who have studied the book-market thoroughly, and as a result they know what is wanted and supply it. Let them have their reward without mean and angry demur.

However one may try to explain the fact, it is none the less true that genuine literature often fails to pay the expenses of publication; at any rate, if it accomplishes more than that, it is infinitesimal as compared with the huge sales of inferior work. I do not know the circulation of Mr Henry Harland's "Comedies and Errors"—possibly it has been moderate—but I would rather be the author of this volume of beautiful workmanship than of all the works of Marie Corelli—the bags of gold notwithstanding. Of course, this is merely a personal preference with which the reader may have no sympathy; but the fact remains that, if a writer produces real literature and it does not sell, he has not therefore failed in his purpose; he may not receive many cheques from his publisher, but it is real compensation to have an audience, "fit though few."

On the general question of literary success, George Henry Lewes says: "We may lay it down, as a rule, that no work ever succeeded, even for a day, but it deserved that success; no work ever failed but under conditions which made failure inevitable. This will seem hard to men who feel that, in their case, neglect arises from prejudice or stupidity. Yet it is true even in extreme cases; true even when the work once neglected has since been acknowledged superior to the works which for a time eclipsed it. Success, temporary or enduring, is the measure of the relation, temporary or enduring, which exists between a work and the public mind."[34]

Failure has a still more fruitful cause—namely, the misdirection of talent. "Men are constantly attempting, without special aptitude, work for which special aptitude is indispensable.

'On peut être honnête homme et faire mal des vers.'

A man may be variously accomplished and yet be a feeble poet. He may be a real poet, yet a feeble dramatist. He may have dramatic faculty, yet be a feeble novelist. He may be a good story-teller, yet a shallow thinker and a slip-shod writer. For success in any special kind of work, it is obvious that a special talent is requisite; but obvious as this seems, when stated as a general proposition, it rarely serves to check a mistaken presumption. There are many writers endowed with a certain susceptibility to the graces and refinements of literature, which has been fostered by culture till they have mistaken it for native power; and these men being destitute of native power are forced to imitate what others have created. They can understand how a man may have musical sensibility, and yet

---

34. "The Principles of Success in Literature,"

not be a good singer; but they fail to understand, at least in their own case, how a man may have literary sensibility, yet not be a good story-teller or an effective dramatist."[35]

The conclusion of the whole matter is this: determine what your projected work is to do; if you are going to offer it in a popular market, give the public plenty for its money, and spice it well; if you are going to offer a sacrifice to the Goddess of Art, be content if you receive no more applause than that which comes from the few worshippers who surround the sacred shrine.

SUCCESS

MINOR CONDITIONS OF SUCCESS

1. Good literature has the same value in manuscript as in typescript, but from the standpoint of author and publisher, it can hardly be said to have the same chances. Penmanship does not tend to improve, and some of the scrawly MSS. sent in to publishers are enough to create dismay in the stoutest heart. It is pure affectation to pretend to be above such small matters. Just as a dinner is all the more appetising because it is neatly and daintily served, so a *MS.* has better chances of being read and appreciated when set out in type-written characters.

2. Be sure that you are sending your *MS.* to the right publisher. Novels with a strongly developed moral purpose are not exactly the kind of thing wanted

---

35. "The Principles of Success in Literature,"

by Mr Heinemann; and if you have anything like "The Woman Who Did," don't send it to a Sunday School Publishing Company. These suppositions are no doubt absurd in the extreme, but they will serve my purpose in pointing out the careless way in which many beginners dispose of their wares. Nearly all publishers specialise in some kind of literature, and it is the novelist's duty to study these types from publishers' catalogues, providing, of course, he does not know them already. The commercial instinct is proverbially lacking in authors; if it were not we should witness less frequently the spectacle of portly MSS. being sent out haphazard to publisher after publisher.

3.   Perhaps my third point ought to have come first. It relates to the obtaining of an expert's views on the matter and form of your story. This will cost you a guinea, perhaps more, but it will save your time and hasten the possibilities of success. You can easily spend a guinea in postage and two or three more in having the MS. re-typed,—and yet the tale be ever the same—"Declined with thanks." Spare yourself many disappointments by putting your literary efforts before a competent critic, and let him point out the crudities, the digressions, and those weaknesses which betray the 'prentice hand. It will not be pleasant to see a pen line through your "glorious" passages, or two blue pencil marks across a favourite piece of dialogue, but it is better to know your de-

fects at once than to discover them by painful and constant rejections.

4.   Be willing to learn; have no fear of hard work; do the best, and write the best that is in you; and never ape anybody, but be yourself.

APPENDICES

Appendix I

The Philosophy of Composition[36]

By Edgar Allan Poe

Charles Dickens, in a note now lying before me, alluding to an examination I once made of the mechanism of "Barnaby Rudge," says—"By the way, are you aware that Godwin wrote his 'Caleb Williams' backwards? He first involved his hero in a web of difficulties, forming the second volume, and then, for the first, cast about him for some mode of accounting for what had been done."

I cannot think this the *precise* mode of procedure on the part of Godwin—and indeed what he himself acknowledges, is not altogether in accordance with Mr. Dickens' idea—but the author of "Caleb Williams" was too good an artist not to perceive the advantage derivable from at least a somewhat similar process. Nothing is more clear than that every plot, worth the name, must be elaborated to its *dénouement* before anything be attempted with the pen. It is only with the *dénouement* constantly in view that we can give a plot its indispensable air of consequence, or causation, by making the incidents, and especially the tone at all points, tend to the development of the intention.

---

36. I do not hold myself responsible for Poe's literary judgments: my purpose in reproducing this essay is to reveal Poe's *methods*.

There is a radical error, I think, in the usual mode of constructing a story. Either history affords a thesis—or one is suggested by an incident of the day—or, at best, the author sets himself to work in the combination of striking events to form merely the basis of his narrative—designing, generally, to fill in with description, dialogue, or authorial comment, whatever crevices of fact, or action, may, from page to page, render themselves apparent.

I prefer commencing with the consideration of an *effect*. Keeping originality *always* in view—for he is false to himself who ventures to dispense with so obvious and so easily attainable a source of interest—I say to myself, in the first place, "Of the innumerable effects, or impressions, of which the heart, the intellect, or (more generally) the soul is susceptible, what one shall I, on the present occasion, select?" Having chosen a novel, first, and secondly a vivid effect, I consider whether it can be best wrought by incident or tone—whether by ordinary incidents and peculiar tone, or the converse, or by peculiarity both of incident and tone—afterward looking about me (or rather within) for such combinations of event, or tone, as shall best aid me in the construction of the effect.

I have often thought how interesting a magazine paper might be written by any author who would—that is to say, who could—detail, step by step, the processes by which any one of his compositions attained its ultimate point of completion. Why such a paper has never been given to the world, I am much at a loss to say—but, perhaps, the authorial vanity has had more to do with the omission than any one other cause. Most writers—poets in especial—prefer having it understood that they compose by a species of fine frenzy—an ecstatic intuition—and would positively shudder at letting the public take a peep behind the scenes, at the elaborate and vacillating crudities of thought—at the true purposes seized only at the last moment—at the innumerable glimpses of idea that arrived not at the maturity of full view—at the fully matured fancies discarded in despair as unmanageable—at the cautious selections and rejections—at the painful erasures and interpolations—in a word, at the wheels and pinions—the tackle for scene-shifting—the stepladders, and demon-traps—the cock's feathers, the red paint and the black patches, which, in ninety-nine cases out of the hundred, constitute the properties of the literary *histrio*.

I am aware, on the other hand, that the case is by no means common, in which an author is at all in condition to retrace the steps by which his conclusions have been attained. In general, suggestions, having arisen pell-mell, are pursued and forgotten in a similar manner.

For my own part, I have neither sympathy with the repugnance alluded to, nor, at any time, the least difficulty in recalling to mind the progressive steps of any of my compositions; and, since the interest of an analysis, or reconstruction, such as I have considered a *desideratum*, is quite independent of any real or fancied interest in the thing analysed, it will not be regarded as a breach of decorum on my part to show the *modus operandi* by which some one of my own works was put together. I select

"The Raven" as most generally known. It is my design to render it manifest that no one point in its composition is referable either to accident or intuition—that the work proceeded, step by step, to its completion with the precision and rigid consequence of a mathematical problem.

Let us dismiss, as irrelevant to the poem, *per se*, the circumstance—or say the necessity—which, in the first place, gave rise to the intention of composing *a* poem that should suit at once the popular and the critical taste.

We commence, then, with this intention.

The initial consideration was that of extent. If any literary work is too long to be read at one sitting, we must be content to dispense with the immensely important effect derivable from unity of impression—for, if two sittings be required, the affairs of the world interfere, and everything like totality is at once destroyed. But since, *cæteris paribus*, no poet can afford to dispense with *anything* that may advance his design, it but remains to be seen whether there is, in extent, any advantage to counterbalance the loss of unity which attends it. Here I say no, at once. What we term a long poem is, in fact, merely a succession of brief ones—that is to say, of brief poetical effects. It is needless to demonstrate that a poem is such, only inasmuch as it intensely excites, by elevating, the soul; and all intense excitements are, through a psychal necessity, brief. For this reason, at least one half of the "Paradise Lost" is essentially prose—a succession of poetical excitements interspersed, *inevitably*, with corresponding depressions—the whole being deprived, through the extremeness of its length, of the vastly important artistic element, totality, or unity, of effect.

It appears evident, then, that there is a distinct limit, as regards length, to all works of literary art—the limit of a single sitting—and that, although in certain classes of prose composition, such as "Robinson Crusoe" (demanding no unity), this limit may be advantageously overpassed, it can never properly be overpassed in a poem. Within this limit, the extent of a poem may be made to bear mathematical relation to its merit—in other words, to the excitement or elevation—again, in other words, to the degree of the true poetical effect which it is capable of inducing; for it is clear that the brevity must be in direct ratio of the intensity of the intended effect:—this, with one proviso—that a certain degree of duration is absolutely requisite for the production of any effect at all.

Holding in view these considerations, as well as that degree of excitement which I deemed not above the popular, while not below the critical, taste, I reached at once what I conceived the proper *length* for my intended poem—a length of about one hundred lines. It is, in fact, a hundred and eight.

My next thought concerned the choice of an impression, or effect, to be conveyed; and here I may as well observe that, throughout the construction I kept steadily in view the design of rendering the work *universally* appreciable. I should be carried too far out of my immediate topic were I to demonstrate a point upon which I have repeatedly insisted, and which, with the poetical, stands not in the slightest need of demonstration—the point, I mean, that Beauty is the sole legitimate province of the poem. A few words, however, in elucidation of my real meaning, which some of my friends have evinced a disposition to misrepresent. That pleasure which is at once the most intense, the most elevating, and the most pure, is, I believe, found in the contemplation of the beautiful. When, indeed, men speak of Beauty, they mean, precisely, not a quality, as is supposed, but an effect—they refer, in short, just to that intense and pure elevation of *soul*—*not* of intellect, or of heart—upon which I have commented, and which is experienced in consequence of contemplating "the beautiful." Now I designate Beauty as the province of the poem, merely because it is an obvious rule of Art that effects should be made to spring from direct causes—that objects should be attained through means best adapted for their attainment—no one as yet having been weak enough to deny that the peculiar elevation alluded to, is *most readily* attained in the poem. Now the object Truth, or the satisfaction of the intellect, and the object Passion, or the excitement of the heart, are, although attainable, to a certain extent, in poetry, far more readily attainable in prose. Truth, in fact, demands a precision, and Passion a*homeliness* (the truly passionate will comprehend me) which are absolutely antagonistic to that Beauty which, I maintain, is the excitement, or pleasurable elevation, of the soul. It by no means follows from anything here said, that passion, or even truth, may not be introduced, and even profitably introduced, into a poem—for they may serve in elucidation, or aid the general effect, as do discords in music, by contrast—but the true artist will always contrive, first, to tone them into proper subservience to the predominant aim; and, secondly, to enveil them, as far as possible, in that Beauty which is the atmosphere and the essence of the poem.

Regarding, then, Beauty as my province, my next question referred to the *tone* of its highest manifestation—and all experience has shown that this tone is one of *sadness*. Beauty of whatever kind, in its supreme development, invariably excites the sensitive soul to tears. Melancholy is thus the most legitimate of all the poetical tones.

The length, the province, and the tone, being thus determined, I betook myself to ordinary induction, with the view of obtaining some artistic piquancy which might serve me as a key-note in the construction of the poem— some pivot upon which the whole structure might turn. In carefully thinking over all the usual artistic effects—or more properly *points*, in the theatrical sense—I did not fail to perceive immediately that no one had been so universally employed as that of the *refrain*. The universality of its employment sufficed to assure me of its intrinsic value, and spared me the necessity of submitting it to analysis. I considered it, however, with regard to its susceptibility of improvement, and soon saw it to be in a primitive condition. As commonly used, the *refrain*, or burden, not only is limited to lyric verse, but depends for its impression upon the force of monotone—both in sound and thought. The pleasure is deduced solely from the sense of identity—of repetition. I resolved to diversi-fy, and so heighten, the effect, by adhering, in general, to the monotone of sound, while I continually varied that of thought: that is to say, I determined to produce contin-uously novel effects, by the variation *of the application* of the *refrain*—the *refrain* itself remaining, for the most part, unvaried.

These points being settled, I next bethought me of the *nature* of my *refrain*. Since its application was to be repeatedly varied, it was clear that the *refrain* itself must be brief, for there would have been an insurmountable difficulty in frequent variations of application in any sen-tence of length. In proportion to the brevity of the sen-tence, would, of course, be the facility of the variation. This led me at once to a single word as the best *refrain*.

The question now arose as to the *character* of the word. Having made up my mind to a *refrain*, the divi-sion of the poem into stanzas was, of course, a corollary: the *refrain* forming the close to each stanza. That such a close, to have force, must be sonorous and susceptible of protracted emphasis, admitted no doubt: and these con-siderations inevitably led me to the long *o* as the most sonorous vowel, in connection with *r* as the most produc-ible consonant.

The sound of the *refrain* being thus determined, it became necessary to select a word embodying this sound, and at the same time in the fullest possible keeping with that melancholy which I had pre-determined as the tone of the poem. In such a search it would have been absolutely impossible to overlook the word "Nevermore." In fact, it was the very first which presented itself.

The next *desideratum* was a pretext for the continuous use of the one word "nevermore." In observing the difficulty which I at once found in inventing a sufficiently plausible reason for its continuous repetition, I did not fail to perceive that this difficulty arose solely from the pre-assumption that the word was to be so continuously or monotonously spoken by *a human* being—I did not fail to perceive, in short, that the difficulty lay in the reconciliation of this monotony with the exercise of reason on the part of the creature repeating the word. Here, then, immediately arose the idea of a *non*-reasoning creature capable of speech; and, very naturally, a parrot, in the first instance, suggested itself, but was superseded forthwith by a Raven, as equally capable of speech, and infinitely more in keeping with the intended *tone*.

I had now gone so far as the conception of a Raven—the bird of ill omen—monotonously repeating the one word, "Nevermore," at the conclusion of each stanza, in a poem of melancholy tone, and in length about one hundred lines. Now, never losing sight of the object *supremeness*, or perfection, at all points, I asked myself—"Of all melancholy topics, what, according to the *universal* understanding of mankind, is the *most* melancholy?" Death—was the obvious reply. "And when," I said, "is this most melancholy of topics most poetical?" From what I have already explained at some length, the answer, here also, is obvious—"When it most closely allies itself to *Beauty*: the death, then, of a beautiful woman is, unquestionably, the most poetical topic in the world—and equally is it beyond doubt that the lips best suited for such topic are those of a bereaved lover."

I had now to combine the two ideas, of a lover lamenting his deceased mistress and a Raven continuously repeating the word "Nevermore."—I had to combine these, bearing in mind my design of varying, at every turn, the *application* of the word repeated; but the only intelligible mode of such combination is that of imagining the Raven employing the word in answer to the queries of the lover. And here it was that I saw at once the opportunity afforded for the effect on which I had been depending—that is to say, the effect of the *variation of application*. I saw that I could make the first query propounded by the lover—the first query to which the Raven should reply "Nevermore"—that I could make this first query a commonplace one—the second less so—the third still less, and so on—until at length the lover, startled from his original *nonchalance* by the melancholy character of the word itself—by its frequent repetition—and by a consideration of the ominous reputation of the fowl that uttered it—is at length excited to superstition, and wildly propounds queries of a far different character—queries whose solution he has passionately at heart—propounds them half in superstition and half in that species of despair which delights in self-torture—propounds them not altogether because he believes in the prophetic or demoniac character of the bird (which, reason assures him, is merely repeating a lesson learned by rote), but because he experiences a frenzied pleasure in so modelling his question as to receive from the *expected* "Nevermore" the most delicious because the most intolerable of sorrow. Perceiving the opportunity thus afforded me—or, more strictly, thus forced upon me in the progress of the construction—I first established in mind the climax, or concluding query—that query to which "Nevermore" should be in the last place an answer—that query in reply to which this word "Nevermore" should involve the utmost conceivable amount of sorrow and despair.

Here then the poem may be said to have its beginning—at the end, where all works of art should begin—for it was here, at this point of my pre-considerations, that I first put pen to paper in the composition of the stanza:

"'Prophet!' said I, 'thing of evil! prophet still, if bird or devil!By that heaven that bends above us—by that God we both adore,Tell this soul with sorrow laden, if, within the distant Aidenn,It shall clasp a sainted maiden whom the angels name Lenore—Clasp a rare and radiant maiden whom the angels name Lenore?'Quoth the Raven, 'Nevermore.'"

I composed this stanza, at this point, first that, by establishing the climax, I might the better vary and graduate, as regards seriousness and importance, the preceding queries of the lover—and, secondly, that I might definitely settle the rhythm, the metre, and the length and general arrangement of the stanza—as well as graduate the stanzas which were to precede, so that none of them might surpass this in rhythmical effect. Had I been able, in the subsequent composition, to construct more vigorous stanzas, I should, without scruple, have purposely enfeebled them, so as not to interfere with the climacteric effect.

And here I may as well say a few words of the versification. My first object (as usual) was originality. The extent to which this has been neglected, in versification, is one of the most unaccountable things in the world. Admitting that there is little possibility of variety in mererhythm, it is still clear that the possible varieties of metre and stanza are absolutely infinite—and yet, *for centuries, no man, in verse, has ever done, or ever seemed to think of doing, an original thing.* The fact is, that originality (unless in minds of very unusual force) is by no means a matter, as some suppose, of impulse or intuition. In general, to be found, it must be elaborately sought, and although a positive merit of the highest class, demands in its attainment less of invention than negation.

Of course, I pretend to no originality in either the rhythm or metre of the "Raven." The former is trochaic—the latter is octameter acatalectic, alternating with heptameter catalectic repeated in the*refrain* of the fifth verse, and terminating with tetrameter catalectic. Less pedantically—the feet employed throughout (trochees) consist of a long syllable followed by a short: the first line of the stanza consists of eight of these feet—the second of seven and a half (in effect two-thirds)—the third of eight—the fourth of seven and a half—the fifth the same—the sixth three and a half. Now, each of these lines, taken individually, has been employed before, and what originality the "Raven" has, is in their *combination into stanza*; nothing even remotely approaching this combination has ever been attempted. The effect of this originality of combination is aided by other unusual, and some altogether novel effects, arising from an extension of the application of the principles of rhyme and alliteration.

The next point to be considered was the mode of bringing together the lover and the Raven—and the first branch of this consideration was the *locale*. For this the most natural suggestion might seem to be a forest, or the fields—but it has always appeared to me that a close *circumscription of space* is absolutely necessary to the effect of insulated incident:—it has the force of a frame to a picture. It has an indisputable moral power in keeping concentrated the attention, and, of course, must not be confounded with mere unity of place.

I determined, then, to place the lover in his chamber—in a chamber rendered sacred to him by memories of her who had frequented it. The room is represented as richly furnished—this in mere pursuance of the ideas I have already explained on the subject of Beauty, as the sole true poetical thesis.

The *locale* being thus determined, I had now to introduce the bird—and the thought of introducing him through the window, was inevitable. The idea of making the lover suppose, in the first instance, that the flapping of the wings of the bird against the shutter, is a "tapping" at the door, originated in a wish to increase, by prolonging, the reader's curiosity, and in a desire to admit the incidental effect arising from the lover's throwing open the door, finding all dark, and thence adopting the half-fancy that it was the spirit of his mistress that knocked.

I made the night tempestuous, first, to account for the Raven's seeking admission, and secondly, for the effect of contrast with the (physical) serenity within the chamber.

I made the bird alight on the bust of Pallas, also for the effect of contrast between the marble and the plumage—it being understood that the bust was absolutely *suggested* by the bird—the bust of *Pallas* being chosen, first, as most in keeping with the scholarship of the lover, and, secondly, for the sonorousness of the word, Pallas, itself.

About the middle of the poem, also, I have availed myself of the force of contrast, with a view of deepening the ultimate impression. For example, an air of the fantastic—approaching as nearly to the ludicrous as was admissible—is given to the Raven's entrance. He comes in "with many a flirt and flutter."

"Not the *least obeisance made he*—not a moment stopped or stayed he, *But, with mien of lord or lady,* perched above my chamber door."

In the two stanzas which follow, the design is more obviously carried out:—

"Then this ebony bird beguiling my sad fancy into smilingBy the *grace and stern decorum of the countenance it wore,*'Though thy *crest be shorn and shaven*, thou,' I said, 'art sure no craven,Ghastly, grim, and ancient Raven wandering from the Nightly shore—Tell me what thy lordly name is on the Night's Plutonian shore?'Quoth the Raven, 'Nevermore.'

Much I marvelled *this ungainly fowl* to hear discourse so plainly,Though its answer little meaning—little relevancy bore;For we cannot help agreeing that no living human being*Ever yet was blessed with seeing bird above his chamber door—Bird or beast upon the sculptured bust above his chamber door,*With such name as 'Nevermore.'"

The effect of the *dénouement* being thus provided for, I immediately drop the fantastic for a tone of the most profound seriousness:—this tone commencing in the stanza directly following the one last quoted, with the line,

"But the Raven, sitting lonely on that placid bust, spoke only," etc.

From this epoch the lover no longer jests—no longer sees any thing even of the fantastic in the Raven's demeanour. He speaks of him as a "grim, ungainly, ghastly, gaunt, and ominous bird of yore," and feels the "fiery eyes" burning into his "bosom's core." This revolution of thought, or fancy, on the lover's part, is intended to induce a similar one on the part of the reader—to bring the mind into a proper frame for the *dénouement*—which is now brought about as rapidly and as*directly* as possible.

With the *dénouement* proper—with the Raven's reply, "Nevermore," to the lover's final demand if he shall meet his mistress in another world—the poem, in its obvious phase, that of a simple narrative, may be said to have its completion. So far, every thing is within the limits of the accountable—of the real. A raven, having learned by rote the single word "Nevermore," and having escaped from the custody of its owner, is driven at midnight, through the violence of a storm, to seek admission at a window from which a light still gleams—the chamber-window of a student, occupied half in poring over a volume, half in dreaming of a beloved mistress deceased. The casement being thrown open at the fluttering of the bird's wings, the bird itself perches on the most convenient seat out of the immediate reach of the student, who, amused by the incident and the oddity of the visitor's demeanour, demands of it, in jest, and without looking for a reply, its name. The raven addressed, answers with its customary word, "Nevermore"—a word which finds immediate echo in the melancholy heart of the student, who, giving utterance aloud to certain thoughts suggested by the occasion, is again startled by the fowl's repetition of "Nevermore." The student now guesses the state of the case, but is impelled, as I have before explained, by the human thirst for self-torture, and in part by superstition, to propound such queries to the bird as will bring him, the lover, the most of the luxury of sorrow, through the anticipated answer "Nevermore." With the indulgence, to the extreme, of this self-torture, the narration, in what I have termed its first or obvious phase, has a natural termination, and so far there has been no overstepping of the limits of the real.

But in subjects so handled, however skilfully, or with however vivid an array of incident, there is always a certain hardness or nakedness, which repels the artistical eye. Two things are invariably required—first, some amount of complexity, or more properly, adaptation; and, secondly, some amount of suggestiveness—some under-current, however indefinite, of meaning. It is this latter, in especial, which imparts to a work of art so much of that *richness* (to borrow from colloquy a forcible term) which we are too fond of confounding with *the ideal*. It is the *excess* of the suggested meaning—it is the rendering this the upper instead of the under current of the theme—which turns into prose (and that of the very flattest kind) the so-called poetry of the so-called transcendentalists.

Holding these opinions, I added the two concluding stanzas of the poem—their suggestiveness being thus made to pervade all the narrative which has preceded them. The under-current of meaning is rendered first apparent in the lines—

"'Take thy beak from out *my heart*, and take thy form from off my door!'Quoth the Raven, 'Nevermore!'"

It will be observed that the words, "from out my heart," involve the first metaphorical expression in the poem. They, with the answer "Nevermore," dispose the mind to seek a moral in all that has been previously narrated. The reader begins now to regard the Raven as emblematical—but it is not until the very last line of the very last stanza, that the intention of making him emblematical of *Mournful and Never-ending Remembrance* is permitted distinctly to be seen:—

"And the Raven, never flitting, still is sitting, still is sitting,On the pallid bust of Pallas, just above my chamber door;And his eyes have all the seeming of a demon's that is dreaming, And the lamplight o'er him streaming throws his shadow on the floor; And my soul *from out that shadow* that lies floating on the floorShall be lifted—nevermore!"

Appendix II

Books Worth Reading

1. "The Art of Fiction." By Sir Walter Besant. Lecture delivered at the Royal Institution, April 25th, 1884.

2. "Le Roman Naturaliste." By F. Brunetiére. Paris, 1883.

3. "The Novel: What it is." By F. Marion Crawford. New York, 1894.

4. "The Development of the English Novel." By W. L. Cross. London, 1899.

5. "Style." By T. de Quincey. "Works." Edinburgh, 1890.

6. "The Limits of Realism in Fiction," and "The Tyranny of the Novel" (in "Questions at Issue"). By Edmund Gosse.

7. "The House of Seven Gables." By N. Hawthorne. See Preface.

8. "Confessions and Criticisms." By Julian Hawthorne.

9. "Criticism and Fiction." By W. D. Howells. New York, 1891.

10. "The Art of Fiction" (in "Partial Portraits"). By Henry James. London, 1888.

11. "The Art of Thomas Hardy." By Lionel Johnson.

12. "The Principles of Success in Literature." By G. H. Lewes. London, 1898.

13. "The English Novel and the Principles of its Development." New York, 1883.

14. "The Philosophy of the Short Story" (in *Pen and Ink*). By Brander Matthews. New York, 1888.

15. "Pierre and Jean." By Guy de Maupassant. See Preface.

16. "Four Years of Novel Reading." By Professor Moulton. London, 1895.

17. "The British Novelists and their Styles." By David Masson. London, 1859.

18. "Appreciations, with an Essay on Style." By Walter Pater. London, 1890.

19. "The English Novel." By Walter Raleigh. London, 1894.

20. "Style." By Walter Raleigh. London, 1897.

21. "The Logic of Style." By W. Renton. London, 1874.

22. "The Philosophy of Fiction." By D. G. Thompson. New York, 1890.

23. "A Humble Remonstrance," and "A Gossip on Ro-

mance" (in "Memories and Portraits"). By R. L. Stevenson.

24. "The Present State of the English Novel" (in "Miscellaneous Essays"). By George Saintsbury. London, 1892.

25. "Notes on Style" (in "Essays: Speculative and Suggestive"). By J. A. Symonds. London, 1890.

26. "The Philosophy of Style." By Herbert Spencer. London, 1872.

27. "Introduction to the Study of English Fiction." By W. E. Simonds. Boston, U.S.A., 1894.

28. "Le Roman Experimental." Paris, 1881.

29. "How to Write Fiction." Published by George Redway.

30. "The Art of Writing Fiction." Published by Wells Gardner.

31. "On Novels and the Art of Writing Them." By Anthony Trollope. In his "Autobiography," vol. ii.

Appendix III

Magazine Articles on Writing Fiction

1. "One Way to Write a Novel." By Julian Hawthorne. *Cosmopolitan*, vol. ii p. 96.

2. "Names in Novels." *Blackwood*, vol cl. p. 230.

3. "Naming of Novels." *Macmillan*, vol. lxi. p. 372.

4. "Fiction as a Literary Form." By H. W. Mabie. *Scribner's Magazine*, vol. v. p. 620.

5. "Candour in English Fiction." By W. Besant, Mrs Lynn Linton, and Thomas Hardy. New Review, vol. ii. p. 6.

6. "The Future of Fiction." By James Sully. *Forum*, vol. ix. p. 644.

7. "Names in Fiction." By G. Saintsbury. Macmillan, vol. lix. p. 115.

8. "Real People in Fiction." By W. S. Walsh. Lippincott, vol. xlviii. p. 309.

9. "The Relation of Art to Truth." By W. H. Mallock. Forum, vol. ix p. 36.

10. "Success in Fiction." By M. O. W. Oliphant. Forum, vol vii. p. 314.

11. "Great Writers and their Art." *Chambers's Journal*, vol. lxv. p. 465.

12. "The Jews in English Fiction." London Quarterly Review, vol. xxviii. 1897.

13. "Heroines in Modern Fiction." National Review, vol. xxix. 1897.

14. "A Claim for the Art of Fiction." By E. G. Wheelwright. Westminster Review, vol. cxlvi. 1896.

15. "The Speculations of a Story-Teller." By G. W. Cable. Atlantic Monthly, vol. lxxviii. 1896.

16. "A Novelist's Views of Novel Writing." By E. S. Phelps. M'Clure's Magazine, vol. viii. 1896.

17. "Hints to Young Authors of Fiction." By Grant Allen. Great Thoughts, vol. vii. 1896.

18. "Novels Without a Purpose." North American Review, vol. clxiii. 1896.

19. "The Fiction of the Future." Symposium. Ludgate Monthly, vol. ii. 1896.

20. "The Place of Realism in Fiction." Humanitarian, vol. vii. 1895. By Dr W. Barry, A. Daudet, Miss E. Dixon, Sir G. Douglas, G. Gissing, W. H. Mallock, Richard Pryce, Miss A. Sergeant, F. Wedmore, and W. H. Wilkins.

21. "The Influence of Idealism in Fiction." By Ingrad Harting. Humanitarian, vol. vi. 1895.

22. "Novelists on their Works." Ludgate Monthly, vol. i. 1895.

23. "Novel Writing and Novel Reading." Interview with Baring Gould. Cassell's Family Magazine, vol. xxii. 1894.

24. "The Women Characters of Fiction." By H. Schutz Wilson. Gentleman's Magazine, vol. cclxxvii. 1894.

25. "School of Fiction Series." In *Atalanta*, vol. vii. 1894:

    1. "The Picturesque Novel, as represented by R. D. Blackmore." By K. Macquoid.

    2. "The Autobiographical Novel, as represented by C. Brontë." By Dr A. H. Japp.

    3. "The Historical Novel, as represented by Sir Walter Scott." By E. L. Arnold.

    4. "The Ethical Novel, as represented by George Eliot." By J. A. Noble.

    5. "The Satirical Novel, as represented by W. M. Thackeray." By H. A. Page.

    6. "The Human Novel, as represented by Mrs Gaskell." By Maxwell Gray.

    7. "The Sensational Novel, as represented by Mrs Henry Wood." By E. C. Grey.

    8. "The Humorous Novel, as represented by Oliver Goldsmith." By Dr A. H. Japp.

26. "The Shudder in Literature." By Jules Claretie. *North American Review*, vol. clv. 1892.

27. "The Profitable Reading of Fiction." By Thomas Hardy. Forum, vol. v. p. 57.

28. "The Picturesque in Novels." Chambers's Journal, vol. lxii. 1892.

29. "Realism in Fiction." By E. F. Benson. Nineteenth Century, vol. xxxiv. 1893.

30. "Great Characters in Novels." Spectator, vol. lxxi. 1893.

31. "The Modern Novel." By A. E. Barr. North American Review, vol. clix. 1894.

32. "The Novels of Adventure and Manners." Quarterly Review, vol. clxxix. 1894.

33. "The Women of Fiction." By H. S. Wilson. Gentleman's Magazine, new series, vol. liii. 1894.

34. "Why do Certain Works of Fiction Succeed?" By M. Wilcox. *New Scientific Review*, vol. i. 1894.

35. "Magazine Fiction, and How not to Write It." By F. M. Bird. Lippincott's Magazine, vol. liv. 1894.

36. "The Picaresque Novel." By J. F. Kelly. New Review, vol. xiii. p. 59.

37. "The Irresponsible Novelist." Macmillan's Magazine, vol. lxxii. p. 73.

38. "Great Realists and Empty Story Tellers." By H. H. Boyesen. *Forum*, vol. xviii. p. 724.

39. "Motion and Emotion in Fiction." By R. M. Doggett. Overland Monthly, new series, vol. xxvi. p. 614.

40. "'Tendencies' in Fiction." By A. Lang. North American Review, vol. clxi. p. 153.

41. "The Two Eternal Types in Fiction." By H. W. Mabie. Forum, vol. xix. p. 41.

42. "The Problem of the Novel." By A. N. Meyer. Arena, vol xvii. 1897.

43. "My Favourite Novel and Novelist." The Munsey Magazine, vols. xvii.-xviii. 1897. By W. D. Howells, B. Matthews, F. B. Stockton, Mrs B. Harrison, S. R. Crockett, P. Bourget, W. C. Russell, and A. Hope Hawkins.

44. "Hard Times among the Heroines of Novels." By E. A. Madden. Lippincott's Magazine, vol. lxix. 1897.

45. "On the Theory and Practice of Local Colour." By W. P. James. Macmillan's Magazine, vol. lxxvi. 1897.

46. "The Writing of Fiction." By F. M. Bird. Lippincott's Magazine, vol. lx. 1897.

47. "Novelists' Estimates of their own Work." National Magazine (Boston, U.S.A.), vol. x. 1897.

48. "Fundamentals of Fiction." By B. Burton. Forum, vol. xxviii. 1899.

49. "On the Future of Novel Writing." By Sir Walter Besant. The Idler, vol. xiii. 1898.

50. "The Short Story." By F. Wedmore. Nineteenth Century, vol. xliii. 1898.

51. "The Complete Novelist." By James Payn. *Strand*, vol. xiv. 1897.

52. "What is a Realist?" By A. Morrison. New Review, vol. xvi. 1897.

53. "The Historical Novel." By B. Matthews. Forum, vol. xxiv. 1897.

54. "The Limits of Realism in Fiction." By Paul Bourget. New Review, vol. viii. p. 201.

55. "New Watchwords in Fiction." By Hall Caine. Contemporary Review, vol. lvii. p. 479.

56. "The Science of Fiction." By Paul Bourget, Walter Besant, and Thomas Hardy. New Review, vol. iv. p. 304.

57. "The Dangers of the Analytic Spirit in Fiction." By Paul Bourget. New *Review*, vol. vi. p. 48.

58. "Cervantes, Zola, Kipling, and Coy." By Brander Matthews. Cosmopolitan, vol. xiv. p. 609.

59. "On Style in Literature." By R. L. Stevenson. Contemporary Review, vol. xlvii. p. 458.

60. "The Apotheosis of the Novel." By Herbert Paul. Contemporary Review, vol. xli. 1897.

61. "Vacant Places in Literature." By W. Robertson Nicoll. British Weekly, March 20, 1895.

62. "What Makes a Novel Successful?" By W. Robertson Nicoll. *British Weekly*, June 16, 1896.

63. "The Use of Dialect in Fiction." By F. H. French. *Atalanta*, vol. viii. p. 125.

Made in the USA
Monee, IL
07 July 2026

56552355R00095